Mastering Drop Shipping Business

Building a Successful Online Retail Empire

Emily Thompson

Table of Contents

INTRODUCTION

Welcome to "Mastering Drop Shipping Business: Building a Successful Online Retail Empire." In the dynamic world of e-commerce, drop shipping stands out as a revolutionary business model that has enabled countless entrepreneurs to launch and grow profitable online stores without the burden of holding inventory. This book is your comprehensive guide to mastering the art and science of drop shipping, equipping you with the knowledge and tools needed to build a thriving online retail empire.

In the following chapters, we will delve deep into every aspect of the drop shipping business, from understanding its fundamental principles to executing advanced strategies for scaling your operations. Whether you are a budding entrepreneur taking your first steps into e-commerce or an experienced retailer looking to expand your horizons, this book provides valuable insights and practical advice tailored to your needs.

You will learn to conduct effective market research, select profitable niches, find reliable suppliers, and set up a compelling online store. Additionally, we will explore essential topics such as marketing, customer conversion, order management, and financial planning. By the end of this book, you will be well-equipped to navigate the challenges of the drop shipping landscape and seize the opportunities that come your way.

Embark on this journey with us, and let's turn your vision of a successful online retail empire into reality. The world of drop shipping awaits—let's master it together.

CHAPTER I

Getting To Know Drop Shipping

What is Drop Shipping?

Drop shipping is a retail fulfillment strategy a retailer uses without holding product inventory. Instead, when a store sells anything, it buys it directly from a third party and ships it straight to the buyer. The merchant never sees or handles the product as a result. The popularity of this business model has increased significantly in recent years, especially with the growth of e-commerce and the increasing number of entrepreneurs seeking to launch enterprises with little initial capital.

Drop shipping is fundamentally a simple procedure. An online retailer receives an order from a consumer. The supplier receives the order data from the store and ships the product to the client, fulfilling the order. While the supplier handles logistics and inventory, the store owner manages marketing and sales as a middleman. Compared to typical retail, when companies buy goods in bulk, store them, and then ship them to clients as orders come in, this strategy stands in stark contrast.

Drop shipping has several benefits, especially for inexperienced business owners. The low setup cost is one of the most significant advantages. Aspiring entrepreneurs can open their stores with less financial risk if they don't have to invest in inventory first. Furthermore, drop shipping gives business owners flexibility by enabling them to function from almost any location with an internet connection. The model also facilitates scalability because the suppliers bear the responsibility for inventory and fulfillment management.

Drop shipping has its challenges, though. Because of the high cost of goods and the fierce competition in online shopping, margins might be small. With less direct product inspection on the store owner's part, quality control and supplier reliability might also be problems. Due to the store owner's need to handle any issues resulting from the supplier's activities, customer service becomes an essential business component. Many business owners have succeeded with drop shipping despite these difficulties by carefully choosing their suppliers, niches, and marketing approaches.

Drop shipping's definition primarily focuses on its application as a fulfillment strategy. This supply chain management strategy involves the retailer sending client orders and shipment information to a manufacturer, another store, or a wholesaler, who ships the items straight to the customer instead of keeping the goods in stock. With this strategy, the products are never seen by the store or handled by them.

Drop shipping entails a few crucial stages. The retailer lists products for sale on their web store. A consumer places an order through the retailer's internet store. The supplier receives the order details from the retailer. The product is shipped straight from the supplier to the client. The merchant oversees customer support and resolves any problems that may come up.

The overhead and operational complexity usually involved in operating a retail firm is decreased by this streamlined method. Retailers can better respond to consumer tastes and market trends by providing more products without worrying about managing and storing inventory.

Over time, drop shipping has seen a substantial evolution. Although drop shipping is a relatively new concept, its foundations may be seen in the late 19th and early 20th-century mail-order catalog companies. These companies would frequently employ a similar business strategy, in which goods were promoted and sold through catalogs, with third parties handling fulfillment.

With the development of e-commerce in the 1990s and the introduction of the internet, drop shipping as we know it today started to take shape. Internet marketplaces such as eBay and Amazon gave small retailers and business owners a way to access a worldwide customer base. Many of these retailers used to store and ship their merchandise. But as e-commerce expanded, so did its complexity and rivalry, which prompted researchers to look into more effective fulfillment strategies.

Specialized drop shipping platforms and services emerged in the early 2000s. Retailers now find it simpler to get products from manufacturers in China and other nations thanks to companies like AliExpress, a member of the Alibaba Group. These platforms offered integrated order fulfillment and delivery technologies and a wide selection of products at low prices.

The drop shipping strategy became widely used in company practices due to the rise of e-commerce platforms like Shopify. With its 2006 introduction, Shopify provided business owners an intuitive framework for building online storefronts. Additionally, it worked with several drop shipping tools, such as Oberlo, to streamline finding products, adding them to an online store, and automating the fulfillment phase.

Digital marketing development has significantly influenced drop shipping companies' success. Search engine marketing, influencer relationships, and social media platforms have made it more affordable for small businesses to connect and interact with prospective clients. Because of these marketing techniques, drop shippers may now compete on an even playing field with bigger, more well-known businesses.

With the development of technology in recent years, the drop-shipping model has continued to change. Artificial intelligence, data analytics, and automation tools are being used to streamline corporate processes, ranging from customer engagement to inventory management. The seamless integration of these technologies has facilitated the effective operation and rapid scaling of drop shipping enterprises.

With continuous advancements in technology and logistics, together with the expansion of e-commerce, drop shipping has a bright future. With the shift in customer behavior towards online buying, especially after the COVID-19 pandemic, there will likely be a greater need for effective and adaptable retail methods such as drop shipping. To be competitive, entrepreneurs venturing into the drop shipping field must keep up with market trends, take advantage of emerging technologies, and iteratively improve their business plans.

Drop shipping offers exceptional potential and obstacles, marking a dramatic change in the conventional retail model. Through comprehension of its definition, historical background, and development, entrepreneurs can more adeptly maneuver through the intricacies of this business model and leverage its potential to establish prosperous e-commerce businesses.

The Drop Shipping Model

Drop shipping is a retail fulfillment technique that has completely changed how companies market their goods. Drop shipping enables retailers to sell goods without maintaining inventory, unlike typical retail models where companies buy and store inventory before selling it to customers. The success of this model depends on suppliers, retailers, and customers working together seamlessly. Each of these parties is essential to the ecosystem.

Drop shipping functions primarily through a simple procedure. A retailer orders a product from a supplier when a customer orders on the retailer's online store. After that, the goods are shipped straight to the customer by the supplier, who keeps the inventory. By doing away with the requirement for the store to handle physical inventory, this procedure lowers overhead expenses and simplifies logistics. The supplier takes care of product storage, packing, and shipping, while the retailer concentrates mainly on marketing, sales, and customer support.

The effectiveness and dependability of a drop shipping company's suppliers are critical to its success. Usually, suppliers are distributors, producers, or wholesalers who offer reduced-cost goods. They are in charge of keeping inventories up to date and fulfilling orders accurately and on schedule. In many instances, suppliers also take care of the product's packaging and delivery to ensure clients receive undamaged orders. Reliable suppliers are essential since any mistakes or delays in the fulfillment process can hurt the retailer's standing and the happiness of its customers. For this reason, building solid connections with reliable suppliers is essential to a flourishing drop shipping company.

The second essential component of the drop shipping concept is retailers, who deal with the public and promote goods to consumers. They design and run internet shops that feature goods purchased from vendors. Retailers are in charge of attracting customers to their stores through various marketing techniques, such as search engine optimization (SEO), social media marketing, paid advertising, and email campaigns. They also handle queries, oversee client relations, and offer post-purchase assistance. A retailer's responsibilities include selecting an appealing product line, producing engaging content, and ensuring customers have a seamless and pleasurable shopping experience. Good merchants set themselves apart with distinctive product offerings, excellent customer support, and a strong sense of brand identity.

The last, but no less significant, participants in the drop shipping concept are the customers. These are the final customers when things are bought from the retailer's online store. The goal of the drop shipping procedure as a whole is to satisfy customers' wants and demands. Consumers anticipate an effortless online shopping experience with clear and accurate product descriptions, competitive pricing, and dependable shipping. Customer satisfaction is critical because satisfied customers are more likely to make repeat purchases, recommend the store to others, and write positive reviews—all of which are critical to the business's success.

How suppliers, merchants, and customers interact with one another defines the drop shipping ecosystem. The seamless coordination of actions amongst these three entities determines the efficacy and efficiency of the model. Retailers must successfully market and sell these products while maintaining top-notch customer service, suppliers must offer high-quality products and dependable delivery services, and customers must receive their orders on time and in the exact condition described.

A more thorough comprehension of the roles and responsibilities within this model emphasizes how crucial cooperation and good communication are. Retailers and suppliers must have explicit agreements regarding product availability, costs, delivery schedules, and return guidelines. Doing this ensures that there are no miscommunications or inconsistencies that can cause problems for the order fulfillment process. Modern technology is essential to making this connection possible. Many drop shipping companies employ platforms and specialized software that interface directly with the inventory systems of their suppliers. This streamlines the process by enabling automated order placing, real-time stock-level updates, and tracking data.

Choosing the appropriate products to sell is critical to the drop shipping business plan. Retailers need to conduct in-depth market research to pinpoint goods with solid demand and manageable profit margins. This entails assessing the competitive environment, comprehending consumer preferences, and studying market trends. To minimize direct competition with larger shops, successful drop shippers frequently concentrate on niche areas where they may offer distinctive or difficult-to-find products.

Customer support is still a vital component of the drop shipping business strategy. Retailers manage the entire customer experience even when not handling the merchandise. This covers resolving any refund concerns, shipment delays, or product quality. To guarantee that customers are happy with their purchases and address any emerging issues, retailers and suppliers must collaborate closely. A retailer's reputation can be significantly improved, and enduring customer loyalty can be developed by offering prompt and efficient customer service.

The development of e-commerce platforms has profoundly altered the drop shipping business model. Online store setup and management have become more straightforward for business owners thanks to platforms like Shopify, WooCommerce, and BigCommerce. These systems frequently have drop shipping connectors built right in, allowing retailers to interact with suppliers, process orders automatically, and run their stores effectively. Furthermore, the emergence of international marketplaces like AliExpress has broadened the selection of products suitable for drop shipping, allowing retailers to procure goods from all over the world.

Although the drop shipping concept has many benefits, there are also drawbacks. Making sure quality control is maintained is one of the main challenges. Retailers depend on suppliers to uphold strict standards because they do not handle the products directly. Any quality drops have the potential to cause unhappy customers and bad reviews. Thus, retailers must be careful to screen their suppliers and keep an eye on the quality of their products.

The drop shipping market's intense competition presents another difficulty. Because there are few entry hurdles, many entrepreneurs can launch drop shipping companies, creating fierce rivalry. Retailers need to stand apart from the competition, whether it's by using cutting-edge marketing techniques, unique product offerings, or excellent customer service. Retailers can differentiate themselves in a competitive market by developing a solid brand and a following of devoted customers.

To sum up, the drop shipping business model is a practical and adaptable approach to managing an online store by capitalizing on the advantages of vendors, buyers, and sellers. Entrepreneurs can create profitable drop shipping companies by knowing their roles and duties and concentrating on customer service, market research, and good communication. The drop shipping model will probably develop and adapt as e-commerce keeps expanding, giving businesses new chances to reach international markets and satisfy customers' shifting needs.

Advantages and Disadvantages

Drop shipping has become a well-liked business strategy, particularly for novice business owners who want to take a low-risk approach to entering the e-commerce market. It has numerous noteworthy benefits, including flexibility, scalability, and inexpensive beginning costs. But it also comes with several serious disadvantages, such as narrow profit margins, fierce rivalry, and unreliable suppliers. Anyone considering drop shipping as a business venture must be aware of these benefits and drawbacks.

The low initial cost of drop shipping is one of its most enormous benefits. Significant upfront investments in inventory, warehousing, and logistics are necessary for traditional retail enterprises. On the other hand, drop shipment does away with these outlays' requirements. Retailers avoid the financial strain of buying stock in bulk because they wait to purchase goods until a customer places an order. Because of this, starting an online store with drop shipping is now a feasible alternative for people with few funds and little risk to their finances. Furthermore, continuous operating costs are much decreased without a physical storefront or warehouse.

Another key advantage of the drop shipping business strategy is flexibility. Retailers have the flexibility to remotely manage their establishments since they may run their enterprises from almost any place with an internet connection. Those who want to live a location-independent lifestyle or operate their business with other obligations may find this freedom incredibly enticing.

Furthermore, retailers may only test out various markets and niches if they take on a lot of financial risk because of the large selection of products offered by drop shipping services. They may move to new items if a particular product or specialty does not do well, so they are not trapped with unsold inventory.

Drop shipping also has the significant benefit of scalability. When scaling, traditional retail organizations frequently encounter major obstacles such as handling more excellent shipping operations, growing storage space, and managing more extensive inventories. These difficulties are handled mainly by the suppliers in drop shipping, freeing up retailers to concentrate on expanding their clientele. Retailers may grow their product lines and penetrate new markets as sales volume rises without overcoming the logistical challenges of raising a company. This expansion is further facilitated by automation tools and software, which streamline operations like order fulfillment and customer support.

Notwithstanding these benefits, drop shipping has several significant drawbacks. Generally speaking, one of the main disadvantages is the low margins. Compared to typical retail models, the cost per item is higher because the retailer does not purchase in bulk. In addition, the market is quite competitive due to the ease of starting drop shipping, frequently resulting in price wars among sellers. This fierce rivalry may make it challenging to attain significant profitability, which can further reduce profit margins. Retailers must stand out from the competition to maintain competitive pricing and guarantee profitability. Effective branding, distinctive product offerings, or first-rate customer service can achieve this.

Another big obstacle in the drop shipping industry is competition. Due to the low entry hurdles, many entrepreneurs can launch drop shipping companies, oversaturating the market with comparable goods. This saturation makes it challenging for a single retailer to stand out. Retailers must keep developing new ideas and invest in solid marketing plans to draw in and keep customers. Overcoming the competitive challenges of drop shipping requires a strong brand and a distinctive value proposition.

The drop shipping strategy poses an essential concern about supplier reliability. The store needs more control over the caliber of goods, packing, and delivery schedules because they rely on other vendors to fulfill their orders. The retailer's reputation and customer satisfaction may be directly impacted by any errors or delays on the supplier's side. Problems like erroneous orders, defective products, or delayed shipments can result in bad press and decreased revenue. Finding trustworthy and dependable providers is so crucial. Retailers must screen possible suppliers carefully, create effective communication channels, and prepare backup plans if supplier concerns crop up.

The absence of inventory control is an additional disadvantage. The retailer relies on the supplier's inventory levels because they do not maintain inventory. This may occur when goods advertised as available on the retailer's website are out of stock, which could cause backorders or cancellations. Customers may become angry about such situations, and the retailer's reputation may suffer. Retailers who want to reduce this risk can work closely with their suppliers and use inventory management systems that offer real-time stock-level updates.

Customer service may also provide more significant difficulties in the drop shipping concept. Resolving consumer complaints regarding product quality or shipment concerns might be more difficult when the store needs to handle the merchandise directly. As a go-between for the supplier and the client, the retailer might need more response times and complicate the settlement process. Effective communication and a solid rapport with suppliers are crucial to guarantee quick and satisfying remedies to client complaints. Retailers should also take the initiative to manage customer expectations by giving accurate and clear product descriptions and reasonable shipment times.

Drop shipping might make branding more challenging. Setting your store apart from the competition and developing a distinctive brand identity might take time because many retailers get their goods from the same suppliers. Custom packaging and private labeling are available, but they cost extra and need more planning. Long-term success in the cutthroat drop shipping business requires developing a solid brand through persistent marketing initiatives, exceptional customer service, and a distinctive value offer.

In conclusion, drop shipping is a popular choice for many business owners due to its numerous alluring benefits, which include inexpensive beginning costs, flexibility, and scalability. But it also comes with many difficulties, such as narrow profit margins, fierce rivalry, and unreliable suppliers. Retailers who want to be successful with drop shipping must carefully negotiate these obstacles by investing in solid marketing and customer service strategies, distinguishing their offers, and choosing trustworthy suppliers. In this fast-paced and cutthroat market, entrepreneurs can create enduring online firms by comprehending and resolving the advantages and disadvantages of drop shipping.

Is Drop Shipping Right for You?

Drop shipping has an irresistible charm. Many prospective entrepreneurs find it appealing as a business model because of its potential for scalable success, inexpensive initial expenses, and little risk. But it's essential to determine if this business strategy is suited for you before jumping into the drop shipping world. This entails knowing the abilities and attitude needed to successfully manage the difficulties and complexities of operating a drop shipping company.

First and foremost, it's critical to understand that drop shipping, like any other commercial endeavor, requires a particular set of talents. Even though drop shipping has a lower entrance barrier than traditional retail, success in the industry demands more than just having an online company. Proficiency in digital marketing is one of the essential talents. Drop shipping primarily depends on online sales; therefore, understanding how to use different marketing methods to increase traffic to your company is crucial. This entails awareness of email campaigns, social media marketing, pay-per-click (PPC) advertising, and search engine optimization (SEO). A store's visibility can be significantly increased, potential customers can be drawn in, and sales can increase with effective digital marketing.

Effective time management and organization abilities are just as crucial as marketing expertise. Drop shipping includes managing customer orders, tracking shipments, liaising with suppliers, and responding to customer care requests. Maintaining organization and effective time management are essential for seamless operations. It takes a skilled multitasker and task prioritizer to maintain the smooth operation of an enterprise. Using software and tools to automate and streamline different procedures can also be beneficial since it frees time to concentrate on strategic growth.

A customer-focused approach is yet another essential component of drop shipping success. The store must deliver exceptional customer service as the primary point of contact for customers. This includes answering questions quickly, handling grievances, and ensuring clients enjoy their shopping experience. Establishing trusting bonds with clients can result in recurring revenue and good word-of-mouth recommendations, essential for sustained success. In a crowded market, a dedication to client pleasure can help your company stand out.

It also helps to have a solid grasp of technology and e-commerce platforms. Setting up and maintaining an online store involves knowledge of BigCommerce, WooCommerce, or Shopify. You may improve your store's functionality and user experience by learning how to utilize these platforms, personalize your store, and incorporate the required tools and apps. Additionally, tracking performance indicators, comprehending consumer behavior, and making well-informed judgments to maximize corporate strategies can all be facilitated by having comfort with data analysis tools.

The mentality needed for drop shipping is just as crucial as the necessary skills. Entrepreneurs need to be resilient and proactive people. In the fiercely competitive world of drop shipping, failures are unavoidable. An optimistic and solution-focused mindset is essential while confronting customer complaints, supplier concerns, or fierce competition. Resilience aids in conquering difficulties and maintaining motivation in the face of setbacks. In the drop shipping market, adaptability and the capacity to learn from mistakes are characteristics of prosperous entrepreneurs.

Perseverance and patience are also essential qualities. It takes time to establish a profitable drop shipping business. Building a consumer base, optimizing your store, and bringing in constant revenue all take consistent work. People who are prepared to put in the time and effort to build their business gradually have a higher chance of success than those who expect instant fame. Long-term gains might result from your persistent efforts to improve company offerings, customer service, and strategy.

Another essential component is a mindset that is open to lifelong learning and evolution. The drop shipping and e-commerce industries are dynamic, with rapidly evolving technologies and trends. Remaining competitive requires keeping abreast of industry advancements, picking up new marketing strategies, and adjusting to shifting consumer tastes. To keep their company current and growing, entrepreneurs must be willing to learn new things and develop their abilities.

It's essential to consider your hobbies and personal interests when determining if drop shipping is appropriate for you. Drop shipping is flexible and can lead to financial independence, but it also takes time and work. A strong passion for the goods you sell or the industry you work in might add to the journey's happiness and fulfillment. Your ability to overcome obstacles, think creatively, and add value for your clients is fueled by passion, which will eventually help your business succeed.

It's crucial to take your risk tolerance into account. Drop shipping reduces the financial risks of inventory management, but it still entails additional hazards, like supplier dependability and market rivalry. It is essential to recognize and acknowledge these risks and implement mitigation plans. The ability to take measured risks and deal with uncertainty will help entrepreneurs better understand the intricacies of the drop shipping business model.

In conclusion, you must carefully consider your abilities, perspective, and personal interests before determining if drop shipping is your best business strategy. Proficiency in digital marketing, excellent organizational skills, a customer-focused mindset, and a firm grasp of e-commerce technologies are essential for success in drop shipping. It's also critical to have a proactive, resilient, and persistent mindset and a constant desire to learn and adapt. Your choice may also be influenced by your enthusiasm for your company and your awareness of your risk tolerance. By carefully weighing these variables, you may decide if drop shipping fits your goals and strengths, which will pave the way for a fulfilling entrepreneurial path.

CHAPTER II

Market Research and Niche Selection

Importance of Market Research

Finding a niche and conducting market research are essential first stages in creating a profitable drop shipping company. Extensive market research lowers risks and boosts chances of success for entrepreneurs by assisting in understanding market demand, target audience identification, and successful niche selection. Comprehending these constituents is vital in formulating efficacious promotional tactics, refining product offers, and establishing the enterprise's competitive standing.

It is impossible to exaggerate the value of market research. It offers insightful information about customer behavior, market trends, and competitive dynamics. Entrepreneurs may make well-informed decisions regarding which things to sell, how much to charge for them, and how best to market them by conducting thorough market research. This study will gather and examine information from various sources, such as market surveys, industry publications, competition analyses, and consumer feedback. Businesses can customize their goods to satisfy customer requests by using this method to detect market gaps, new trends, and unmet wants.

An essential component of market research is comprehending consumer demand. The amount of a good or service buyers are willing and able to buy at a specific price is called market demand. Businesses can decide whether a product has enough interest to warrant its inclusion in their inventory by accurately estimating market demand. There are various techniques for determining market demand. One method is to use keyword research tools or Google Trends, which offer information on the popularity of particular search phrases over time, to study search trends. This data can show if consumer interest in a given product is rising, falling, or staying the same.

Analyzing sales data from internet marketplaces like Amazon, eBay, and AliExpress is another way to determine market demand. These platforms frequently offer data on top-selling items, client testimonials, and sales rankings, all of which can give important insights into customers' preferences and purchasing habits. Social media sites like Facebook, Pinterest, and Instagram are also helpful for tracking consumer conversations and trending products. Businesses can find popular products and learn more about what interests customers by watching these sites.

Another crucial part of market research is determining target consumers. A specific group of customers who are most likely to be interested in a given good or service is known as the target audience. Segmenting the market according to various criteria, including buying habits, psychographics, location, and demographics, defines a target audience. Businesses can effectively reach and engage consumers by customizing their marketing techniques to identify and understand their target population.

Demographic segmentation pertains to the market division based on attributes like age, gender, income, occupation, and level of education. For instance, a company that sells expensive exercise gear would target well-to-do individuals between the ages of 25 and 45 who value their health and have extra money to spend. Contrarily, psychographic segmentation concentrates on the target audience's attitudes, values, interests, and lifestyles. Businesses may craft marketing messages that connect with their target audience's values and goals by thoroughly understanding psychographic characteristics. For example, a company that sells eco-friendly goods might go after customers who value sustainability and are concerned about the environment.

Targeting customers according to their location is known as geographic segmentation. This may be especially helpful for companies that sell goods tailored to the needs or preferences of a particular area. For instance, a shop of equipment for winter activities would concentrate its marketing efforts on areas with chilly climates and well-liked skiing areas. Behavioral segmentation considers customers' purchasing habits, including frequency of purchases, brand loyalty, and product consumption. Businesses can spot trends in previous consumer behavior and adjust their marketing tactics to promote recurring business and brand loyalty.

Selecting a particular market segment to concentrate on is known as niche selection, and it is strongly associated with market research. Choosing the correct niche is essential to stand out in the crowded drop shipping market. A well-selected niche enables companies to focus on a particular customer base with specialized offerings and marketing approaches, which facilitates the development of a strong brand identity and a devoted following. When choosing a niche, businesses should consider variables, including market demand, competitiveness, profitability, and personal interest.

When selecting a niche, market demand is the main factor to consider. A highly sought-after niche suggests a sufficient number of prospective buyers interested in the offerings. But it's also critical to consider how competitive the specialty is. It can take much work to break into highly competitive niches, particularly for new enterprises. Businesses can find chances for differentiation and learn about the advantages and disadvantages of their rivals by doing a competitive study.

Another important consideration when choosing a specialty is profitability. Companies should assess a niche's possible profit margins by considering variables, including product costs, pricing policies, and delivery costs. Specific niches may be in great demand, but they may not be profitable because of tight margins or fierce competition. However, niches with larger profit margins might provide more significant potential for expansion and long-term viability.

A person's passion and areas of interest are also important considerations when choosing a specialty. Choosing a specialty that fits personal interests can make the trip more exciting and encouraging. Running a business involves dedication and perseverance. Long-term success can be facilitated by innovation, improved consumer interaction, and a passion for the products and the industry.

In summary, conducting market research and choosing a specialty are crucial in creating a profitable drop shipping company. Businesses can use market research to make well-informed decisions about their product offers and marketing strategies by gaining insightful knowledge about consumer behavior, market demand, and competition dynamics. While identifying target audiences enables firms to customize their marketing efforts to reach and engage consumers, understanding market demand successfully helps them find profitable items and avoid risks. Selecting a niche in the market is deciding which particular area to concentrate on while considering demand, competition, profitability, and personal interest. In the cutthroat world of drop shipping, businesses can position themselves for success by carefully choosing their specialty and completing in-depth market research.

Tools and Techniques for Market Research

Market research is a crucial component in creating a profitable drop shipping company. Data must be gathered and analyzed to comprehend customer behavior, market demand, and competitive dynamics. The efficiency of market research can be significantly increased by utilizing a variety of instruments and methodologies, which offer insightful information that helps guide business strategy. Keyword research, competitor analysis, and Google Trends are necessary instruments and methods for market research.

A valuable tool for assessing consumer demand and spotting long-term patterns is Google Patterns. It offers information on how popular search phrases are in various locations and periods. By examining this data, entrepreneurs can see new trends, seasonal fluctuations, and regional disparities in consumer interest. For instance, you can use Google Trends to analyze how search terms like "yoga mats" or "home gym equipment" have evolved over the previous year if you're considering selling fitness equipment. This will enable you to assess whether consumer interest in these products increases or decreases. Furthermore, Google Trends lets you analyze several search keywords at once, making it easier to determine which products are in greater demand than others.

Another critical method in market research is keyword research, especially when finding out what prospective buyers are searching for online. Comprehensive search traffic, competition, and keyword difficulty data may be obtained with tools like Ahrefs, SEMrush, and Google Keyword Planner. By examining these indicators, businesses may find low-competition, high-demand keywords that can help them rank higher in search engine results and drive more traffic to their websites. Investigating both long-tail and short-tail keywords is part of keyword research. Broad search terms like "shoes" or "electronics," which usually have substantial search volumes but also intense competition, are examples of short-tail keywords. More specialized terms, like "best running shoes for women" or "affordable gaming laptops," are long-tail keywords. Because they often have lower search volume but less competition, they are easier to target in specialist industries.

Businesses may enhance search engine optimization (SEO) and provide content that reflects customer interests by comprehending the subtleties of keyword research. Companies can improve their search engine exposure, draw in more organic visitors, and increase sales by adding pertinent keywords to product descriptions, blog articles, and other website content. In addition, keyword research can identify associated terms and phrases that prospective buyers use, offering insights into product possibilities and content ideas.

An essential component of market research is competition analysis, which entails assessing the advantages and disadvantages of current rivals. This method aids companies in comprehending the competitive environment, spotting market gaps, and creating unique strategies. Tools like SimilarWeb, SpyFu, and BuzzSumo may give you comprehensive data on the backlinks, keywords, social media activity, and competitors' website traffic. By examining this data, businesses can learn about their competitors' product lines, marketing plans, and customer service techniques.

Finding out who your rivals are is one of the first steps in competition analysis. This entails examining companies that cater to the same clientele or provide comparable goods. Once located, you can explore their websites to learn about their offerings, costs, and marketing tactics. Please take note of their website's layout and user experience in addition to the caliber of their writing. This might provide insights on what appeals to users and how to improve your website.

It's also critical to assess the marketing tactics of rival companies. Examine their social media accounts to find out what content they share, how frequently they post, and how their followers interact with it. You may find the most effective content pieces they have produced using tools like BuzzSumo, which can serve as inspiration for your content marketing campaigns. Additionally, you can improve your SEO methods by studying your competitors' keywords and backlink profiles.

Gaining helpful insights can also come from analyzing competitors' consumer evaluations and feedback. Through perusing client testimonials on rival websites and independent review sites like Yelp and Amazon, you can spot frequent grievances and opportunities for development. By using this information, you may improve your product line and customer support, giving your customers a better experience than your rivals.

Your company plan can significantly improve by including competitor analysis, keyword research, and Google Trends information in your market research process. By thoroughly grasping customer behavior, market demand, and competition dynamics, these tools and strategies help you make well-informed pricing, marketing, and product selection decisions.

For instance, if keyword analysis reveals substantial search volumes and little competition for terms like "biodegradable phone cases" and Google Trends shows a growing interest in eco-friendly products, this could be a lucrative area to explore. Analyzing competitors may show that there is room for difference in this market due to subpar customer service or a narrow selection of products offered by current vendors.

Combining these insights allows you to create a unique value offer that meets consumer needs and distinguishes you from rivals. This could entail expanding your selection of environmentally friendly phone cases, giving top-notch customer support, and utilizing focused keywords to boost your SEO and draw in organic visitors.

Furthermore, ongoing market research is necessary to maintain competitiveness in the ever-changing world of e-commerce. Rapid changes in consumer preferences and trends call for constant analysis to make sure you stay adaptable. You may keep ahead of the competition and find fresh growth prospects by routinely checking Google Trends, researching new keywords, and updating your competitor analysis.

Successful market research is essential to a drop shipping company's success. Competitive dynamics, customer behavior, and market demand can all be understood using technologies such as Google Trends, keyword research platforms, and competitor analysis tools. Businesses can position themselves for long-term success, make well-informed decisions, and maximize their strategy by utilizing these tools and practices. In addition to assisting in identifying lucrative niches and comprehending target markets, market research helps organizations remain adaptable and flexible in a constantly changing industry.

Selecting a Profitable Niche

Selecting the appropriate niche is essential in creating a profitable drop shipping company. A niche is a specific area of the market reserved for a particular class of goods or services. Carefully weighing several factors, such as market need, competitiveness, profitability, and personal interest, is necessary when choosing a lucrative niche. To ensure that the company is financially feasible and long-term rewarding and sustainable, it is imperative to strike a balance between passion and profitability.

Market demand serves as the primary selection criterion for niches. It's crucial to know whether there is enough demand for a product. Even the most effective marketing plans will result in sales with demand. Entrepreneurs can examine the popularity of search terms associated with their potential niche using tools such as Google Trends to determine the market demand level. Furthermore, keyword research tools like Ahrefs, SEMrush, and Google Keyword Planner can provide information on the volume and patterns of searches for particular products. A high search volume indicates strong demand, and long-term trends suggest steady interest. Analyzing sales data from online retailers like Amazon and eBay is also helpful since it can highlight popular products and categories.

Another essential thing to think about is competition. Breaking into a highly competitive niche might be challenging, especially for novices. Staying out in a crowded market is brutal, brewing price wars and narrowing profit margins. As a result, determining the degree of rivalry within a niche is crucial. A competitive analysis can examine the number of competitors, their market share, and their advantages and disadvantages. Competitors' traffic and marketing tactics can be analyzed using tools like SimilarWeb and SpyFu. Entrepreneurs should ideally target markets with moderate levels of competition, where there is potential for difference while still having a reasonable level of demand.

Profitability is still another critical factor. Specific markets may have strong demand but thin profit margins, making it challenging to provide a steady income. Entrepreneurs should consider variables, including product cost, pricing tactics, shipping costs, and likelihood of repeat business when assessing profitability. More excellent marketing and price freedom are possible for products with significant profit margins. Long-term profitability can also be improved by offering products that promote repurchases, such as consumables or goods with a high upselling potential. A niche's financial viability must be ascertained by computing prospective earnings after deducting all expenditures and comparing the results to anticipated revenue.

The accessibility of providers and the quality of their offerings are crucial factors to consider. Locating trustworthy suppliers who provide high-quality goods, affordable costs, and dependable shipping is essential for a drop shipping company. Unsatisfactory supplier performance can harm the company's reputation and cause customer displeasure. Business owners should carefully screen prospective suppliers, who should look at their ratings, reviews, and past performance. Online marketplaces like Oberlo, SaleHoo, and AliExpress can help identify and assess vendors. Achieving seamless operations and customer satisfaction can be facilitated by building good relationships with suppliers and keeping lines of communication open.

Choosing a niche might be difficult, but balancing enthusiasm and profitability is essential. Although monetary success is crucial, operating a business on one's hobbies and interests can foster creativity, motivation, and fulfillment. Entrepreneurs who are enthusiastic about their industry are likelier to put in the time and effort required to overcome obstacles and advance their company. A more accurate and captivating brand story may be created by genuine excitement and product expertise, which can further increase customer engagement.

But it's crucial to find a balance between enthusiasm and financial success. A profitable firm cannot survive in a niche that interests you but has little demand. On the other hand, burning out and losing motivation may result from a very lucrative specialty you are not interested in. Therefore, it's crucial to identify a niche that complements your passions and offers market potential. List your interests, pastimes, and areas of competence first. Then, look into the competitors and market demand for similar products. This method assists in locating profitable and personally fulfilling niches.

If you are interested in health and fitness, look into markets for yoga mats, home workout gear, or dietary supplements. You can examine competition and demand in these domains using market research tools. You discover a reasonable level of competition and an increasing demand for yoga mats. If you know a lot about and are passionate about yoga, this can be a good niche for you to pursue your business dreams.

While choosing a niche, it's also advantageous to consider sustainability in the long run. While they might not offer long-term prospects, trends, and fads can be quite profitable in the short run. Seek out markets with stable demand and room to expand. Long-term viable niches can be found by analyzing customer behavior and broader market trends. For example, the growing consciousness about sustainability and environmental challenges can turn eco-friendly items into a lucrative and enduring market niche.

Engaging with your target audience can also yield insightful information and validate your choice of specialization. Engage in social media groups, online forums, and communities associated with your possible niche to gain insight into your target audience's needs, preferences, and pain points. Direct communication with prospective clients can help you hone your product offerings and marketing plans so your target market will find them appealing.

In conclusion, choosing a lucrative specialty for a drop shipping company necessitates considering factors including supplier dependability, profitability, market demand, and rivalry. It's crucial to balance passion and revenue to ensure the company can support itself financially and provide personal fulfillment. Through the use of tools and procedures for market research, an assessment of sustainability over the long term, and interaction with the target audience, entrepreneurs can determine which niches have the highest potential for success. A well-selected niche offers a fulfilling and pleasurable entrepreneurial experience and increases the likelihood of business success.

Validating Your Niche Idea

Building a profitable drop shipping company requires several steps, one of which is validating a niche concept. It entails evaluating a product or niche's viability to ensure it offers potential for profitability and satisfies market demand. Before devoting substantial time and resources to a niche idea, entrepreneurs can lower risks and improve the chances of success by verifying the concept. Market research, product testing, feedback collection, and iteration based on insights are crucial in determining whether a product is viable.

A niche idea's validation starts with market research. It aids business owners in comprehending the competition, target market, and customer preferences. Business owners can pinpoint possibilities and obstacles specific to their selected specialty by examining industry trends, search traffic, and competition strategies. Google Trends, keyword research platforms, and competitor analysis tools offer insights into market demand and competitive dynamics. By conducting market research, business owners may learn more about their target market's wants, needs, and pain points, which will help them choose products and develop marketing plans.

After conducting market research to identify a possible niche idea, testing product feasibility is the next stage. This entails choosing niche-specific products and evaluating their function in the marketplace. Starting a drop shipping store can involve an entrepreneur sourcing a limited number of products from suppliers and listing them. Through tracking engagement indicators, sales, and customer feedback, business owners can evaluate the level of demand for their products and their potential profitability. Entrepreneurs can assess the performance of their products by using tools such as Google Analytics and the built-in analytics of e-commerce platforms, which offer helpful information on website traffic, conversion rates, and customer behavior.

Customer feedback is crucial for refining product offerings and verifying niche ideas. Numerous platforms, such as social media interaction, product reviews, and client surveys, can be used. Entrepreneurs can learn about their consumers' preferences, problems, and ideas for change by asking for feedback. By focusing on client feedback, business owners may pinpoint the advantages and disadvantages of their products, improve their services, and elevate the overall customer experience. Additionally, entrepreneurs may develop relationships, encourage loyalty, and gain insights into industry trends and consumer behavior by interacting directly with customers through social media platforms and email marketing.

Validating a niche idea requires iterating based on insights from market research and client feedback. This entails regularly improving price plans, marketing campaigns, and product offers in light of consumer preferences and data-driven insights. Entrepreneurs may meet client wants, adjust to shifting market conditions, and outperform rivals by continuously developing and iterating. Enterprising individuals might enhance their chances of success by experimenting with various product variations, pricing schemes, and promotional platforms. Furthermore, being adaptable and receptive to criticism helps business owners make swift adjustments in reaction to market developments and new opportunities.

An entrepreneur is testing a specialized market for environmentally friendly household cleaning supplies. After gathering supplier quotes and performing market research, they list these items on their drop shipping site. They find that some products, like reusable cleaning cloths and natural disinfectant sprays, are very well-liked by consumers by keeping an eye on sales and customer comments. In response to this feedback, the business owner chooses to concentrate on these high-performing items and increase their product line within the eco-friendly house cleaning niche. They also test out various price and marketing approaches to further hone their plan.

To sum up, one of the most critical steps in creating a profitable drop shipping company is to validate a specialized idea. Entrepreneurs can ensure that their selected niche has potential for profitability and meets market needs by gathering feedback, evaluating the feasibility of their product, and iterating based on those findings. Product selection and marketing strategies are informed by the valuable insights that market research offers about consumer preferences, competition, and market trends. Various products must be sourced to determine demand and profitability, and sales, customer reviews, and engagement data must be tracked. By getting client feedback, business owners may improve the overall customer experience, pinpoint the strengths and shortcomings of their products, and iterate on their services. By iterating based on insights, entrepreneurs maximize their chances of success, respond to shifting market conditions, and meet client wants. Entrepreneurs can position themselves for long-term growth and profitability in the cutthroat drop shipping market by taking the following steps to prove their specialized ideas.

CHAPTER III

Finding Reliable Suppliers

Types of Suppliers

Getting trustworthy suppliers is essential to operating a profitable business. Suppliers maintain the flow of required goods and materials, which affects everything from manufacturing schedules to the quality of finished goods. Making educated sourcing decisions requires an understanding of the many kinds of suppliers and the differences between domestic and foreign sources, as well as between manufacturers and wholesalers.

Regarding supplier types, manufacturers and distributors are the two main groups. The companies that turn raw materials into finished things are known as manufacturers. They supply goods straight from the source and are the starting point of the production chain. By collaborating with manufacturers, companies can tailor their products to meet specific requirements and create a distinctive product offering. Since there are no middlemen to drive up expenses, this direct interaction may result in better pricing. Manufacturers can also offer insights into the production process, which is very helpful for innovation and quality assurance.

Conversely, wholesalers serve as a middleman between retailers and final customers or producers. They buy products in bulk from producers and resell them to companies in smaller amounts. Convenience is the main benefit of working with wholesalers. They frequently keep an extensive range of goods in store from several manufacturers, acting as a one-stop shop for companies needing to source numerous products. Since wholesalers usually maintain inventory, they can also provide quicker delivery times. But occasionally, the extra layer separating procurement and production can lead to increased expenses and less direct communication about product specifications and manufacturing procedures.

Selecting between local and foreign vendors introduces yet another level of difficulty. Domestic suppliers, or those based in the same nation as the company making the purchase, have various benefits. Shorter shipping times are usually necessary to fulfill production deadlines and maintain inventory levels. Due to the lack of language barriers and the greater familiarity with business procedures, communication is frequently more direct. In addition to reducing risks related to product quality and legal concerns, working with domestic suppliers can offer a degree of assurance regarding compliance with local laws and norms.

However, domestic providers could have higher fees because local labor and production costs are higher. This is the point when using foreign suppliers becomes appealing. Suppliers with headquarters in nations with lower labor costs can provide noticeably less expensive goods, drastically cutting production costs. Furthermore, access to items or resources that are not easily found domestically is often made possible by overseas marketplaces, expanding the options open to companies wanting to innovate or diversify.

However, overseas sourcing presents a unique set of difficulties. Linguistic obstacles and cultural differences in the workplace might impede communication. Customs procedures and foreign logistics increase the likelihood of delays and lengthen shipping durations. Quality control can also be more challenging, necessitating more frequent inspections and stricter due diligence. Exchange rate volatility and geopolitical unrest can also raise financial concerns that must be adequately controlled.

A calculated approach is needed to balance these factors. For example, a company may import completed goods from overseas vendors to save money but source raw materials domestically to guarantee quality and prompt delivery. This hybrid strategy can maximize advantages while reducing risks.

The decision between manufacturers and wholesalers frequently comes down to the particular requirements and competencies of the company. Because wholesalers offer a more comprehensive selection of products at lower minimum order quantities, they may be more advantageous for startups and small businesses. Establishing direct partnerships with manufacturers may benefit larger organizations with specialized product requirements and greater purchasing power. This is because manufacturers can negotiate better prices and adapt items to meet specific needs.

Whether a manufacturer or a distributor, establishing a trustworthy supply base takes careful investigation and due attention. Assessing a potential supplier's production capability, quality control procedures, financial stability, and market standing are all critical aspects of the evaluation process. Trial orders, recommendations from previous customers, and site inspections can all offer insightful information about a supplier's dependability.

To sum up, locating trustworthy suppliers requires a thorough grasp of the many kinds of providers out there and the advantages and disadvantages of sourcing domestically vs globally. While wholesalers offer a wide selection of products and convenience, manufacturers have direct access to production and customizing opportunities. While overseas suppliers can provide significant cost reductions but come with additional risks, domestic suppliers guarantee faster lead times and better communication, but frequently at higher rates. By carefully weighing these elements, businesses can create a strong supplier strategy that supports their operational requirements and strategic objectives.

How to Find Suppliers

Locating trustworthy suppliers is essential for companies looking to keep a constant supply of high-quality goods and supplies. With the development of globalization and technology, sourcing strategies have changed dramatically, and it is now critical for companies to comprehend and use various channels. Online directories, trade exhibitions, and networking are essential techniques that offer distinct benefits and methods for finding suppliers.

Online directories are becoming among the most helpful and readily available resources for locating suppliers. These directories gather large lists of producers, distributors, and service providers, frequently divided into categories based on the industry, kind of product, and region. Thanks to their extensive databases and intuitive interfaces, platforms such as Global Sources, Thomas Net, and Alibaba are well-known for facilitating speedy supplier searches and enterprise comparisons. One of the main advantages of online directories is the ability to filter searches based on particular criteria, such as minimum order quantities, certifications, and prior customer ratings. This specificity helps companies reduce the time and effort needed to discover acceptable partners by assisting them to focus their selections on vendors who fulfill their unique criteria.

Numerous internet directories provide valuable resources, including buying guides, industry news, forums where companies may exchange experiences and insights, and search functions. These characteristics can give additional context and support better decision-making for organizations. Although online directories are comprehensive and convenient, careful research is still necessary. Ensuring that online profiles correspond with reality requires crucial actions, including confirming the legitimacy of suppliers, vetting references, and scheduling site visits or third-party inspections.

Another excellent way to locate suppliers is through trade events, which provide a more hands-on and engaging experience than internet searches. These gatherings create a vibrant networking and business development atmosphere by bringing together many suppliers, industry professionals, and prospective customers. Trade exhibitions that offer unrivaled chances to learn about new products and technologies, such as the Canton Fair in China, CES in the United States, and Hannover Messe in Germany, draw thousands of exhibitors and attendees worldwide.

Trade exhibitions offer a unique opportunity for direct communication with suppliers, a value that cannot be overstated. In-person contacts provide a more nuanced understanding of a potential partner's dependability and professionalism. The chance to personally view, feel, and judge products is invaluable in determining their appropriateness and quality. Demonstrations, seminars, and workshops held during trade exhibits offer additional insights into industry trends and best practices, enriching the audience's understanding and making them feel more confident in their supplier assessment.

However, a considerable time and financial commitment is involved in attending trade events. Particularly for smaller enterprises, travel costs, registration fees, and the requirement for sufficient preparation might be significant. It is essential to conduct before research on the event, identify important exhibitors and sessions, and establish specific goals to optimize the advantages. When trade exhibitions are planned well, time spent there is productive and aligned with company objectives.

Another essential strategy for locating suppliers is networking, which uses connections and relationships to identify trustworthy providers. Professional affiliations, trade associations, and casual relationships like friends, family, and coworkers can all be considered part of a business network. Compared to anonymous internet reviews, these networks frequently offer suggestions and referrals based on firsthand knowledge, which might be more reliable.

Attending networking events tailored to your industry, such as conferences, workshops, and business mixers, can help you meet new people and connect with possible suppliers. Your exposure and reputation in the business can be improved by actively participating in these events, whether by speaking on panels, presenting a presentation, or just having talks. Furthermore, social media sites such as LinkedIn have effective networking capabilities that let you contact business people in the field, join groups that interest you, and participate in conversations that may result in supplier referrals.

Developing a solid network takes time and energy; you must be willing to assist individuals in your network and interact consistently. Adding value—for example, by sharing knowledge, making recommendations, or working together on projects—may fortify connections and foster an atmosphere where people are more likely to assist you in your supplier search.

To summarize, locating suppliers entails utilizing a blend of web directories, trade exhibitions, and networking to establish a dependable and varied supplier pool. Online directories are a handy place to start when looking for suppliers because they provide readily available information. Trade exhibitions demand a sizeable financial commitment but offer direct interaction and an initial assessment of goods and suppliers. By connecting with people on a personal and professional level, networking provides dependable referrals and the chance to create enduring relationships. By strategically applying these techniques, companies may successfully negotiate the intricate terrain of supplier sourcing, guaranteeing that they identify collaborators who satisfy their demands for dependability, affordability, and quality.

Evaluating Suppliers

Supplier evaluation is a critical element of supply chain management that significantly impacts a company's productivity and output quality. Choosing trustworthy and superior providers necessitates a thorough evaluation based on predetermined standards. Moreover, sustaining a robust and effective supply chain depends on developing solid connections with suppliers.

Precise standards for dependability and excellence must be established to begin assessing suppliers. A supplier's dependability is usually evaluated by their capacity to deliver goods in the right quantities, on schedule, and by specifications. A dependable provider should demonstrate a history of accuracy and timeliness in order fulfillment. Performance data, records, and client comments can all be used to assess this. Key performance indicators (KPIs) such as lead time variability, order correctness, and the rate of on-time delivery are crucial to consider.

Another essential factor is quality, which includes the standards and procedures a supplier follows and the caliber of the goods they provide. Suppliers must adhere to industry norms and hold pertinent certifications, such as ISO 9001, for quality control systems. This guarantees that the provider maintains product quality by following methodical procedures. It is essential to assess a supplier's quality control procedures, including handling faults, monitoring manufacturing, and inspecting raw materials. Visiting the locations or hiring outside auditors might get a firsthand look at these procedures.

Another crucial factor in the assessment of suppliers is their financial soundness. A financially secure supplier is more likely to be dependable and able to increase output as necessary. A supplier's economic situation can be ascertained by looking into their financial records, credit history, and length of operation. Furthermore, evaluating the supplier's capacity and scalability is critical, especially if your company expects growth or erratic demand. A provider needs to increase output without sacrificing timeliness or quality.

Transparency and communication are other important considerations when assessing vendors. Good communication ensures everyone is on the same page about deadlines, specs, and expectations. Providers are more likely to cultivate a reliable relationship if they are transparent about their procedures, problems, and updates. Their degree of cooperation and transparency can be determined by assessing how quickly they respond and how willing they are to share specific information.

Long-term success depends on establishing trusting connections with qualified suppliers after they have been found. Strong supplier relationships promote cooperation, trust, and mutual development in addition to transactional exchanges. Effective communication is one of the main strategies for developing these kinds of connections. Maintaining open lines of communication regularly ensures that concerns are addressed quickly and that everyone is informed of any changes to standards or expectations. A continual conversation and improved understanding between parties can be maintained by scheduling frequent meetings, performance evaluations, and feedback sessions.

Any healthy connection starts with trust. Establishing trust with suppliers requires exhibiting dependability, honesty, and respect for one another. Building this trust can be facilitated by keeping word, paying bills on schedule, and being open and honest about business goals and difficulties. However, suppliers should also show they are dependable by continuously living up to expectations and taking the initiative to address problems.

Building solid supplier connections also requires collaboration. This entails cooperating to find solutions, enhance procedures, and create new ideas. As an illustration, involving suppliers in product development can result in more effectively designed goods and more productive manufacturing procedures. Additionally, cooperative projects that benefit both parties, like sustainability initiatives or cooperative cost-saving projects, can fortify the partnership.

It's crucial to acknowledge and honor excellent work as well. Recognizing suppliers' efforts and accomplishments can inspire them to uphold high standards and promote a positive working relationship. Programs for prizes, recognition, and incentives based on performance can strengthen a supplier's dedication to quality.

Furthermore, in supplier partnerships, adaptation and flexibility are crucial. In times of crisis, especially, businesses should be ready to grant suppliers' legitimate requests to modify order schedules or payment terms. Strengthening the relationship and fostering loyalty can be accomplished by exhibiting compassion and understanding throughout trying times.

Furthermore, risk management is essential to preserving solid supplier relationships. The identification and development of contingency plans can aid in mitigating potential risks, such as financial instability, geopolitical concerns, and supply disruptions. Preparation is ensured, and the impact of unanticipated events is reduced by routinely assessing and revising these plans with input from suppliers.

To sum up, assessing suppliers entails comprehensively evaluating their dependability, quality, financial stability, communication, and scalability. These standards aid in identifying vendors who can reliably and highly competently satisfy a company's needs. Strong supplier relationships need constant trust, cooperation, acknowledgment, communication, and adaptability. By cultivating these partnerships, businesses can build a robust supply chain that promotes mutual growth and long-term success. In addition to improving operational effectiveness, efficient supplier management fosters innovation and competitive advantage.

Negotiating Terms and Prices

For companies looking to maximize their supply chain operations and guarantee profitability, negotiating terms and prices with suppliers is an essential talent. A strategic strategy that considers the long-term relationship, contractual commitments, and immediate financial terms is necessary for effective negotiation. Since contracts and agreements define conditions and protect the interests of both parties, it is equally crucial to understand the nuances of these legal instruments.

The first step in every successful negotiation approach is careful planning. It is essential to conduct in-depth research on the supplier, market conditions, and industry standards before beginning negotiations. Knowledge of the supplier's cost structure, production capacity, and financial status can give you significant negotiating influence. Furthermore, comparing terms and pricing to industry averages aids in establishing reasonable expectations and pointing out potential areas for concessions.

Setting specific goals is yet another essential component of preparing for negotiations. Companies should list their top goals, which include lowering prices, extending payment periods, enhancing quality standards, or improving delivery timetables. It is easier to stay focused and guarantee that essential needs are not compromised during negotiating when one is aware of what is and is not negotiable.

Establishing a good relationship with the supplier is crucial to successful negotiating. A constructive and cooperative connection can facilitate mutual understanding and open communication. Finding win-win solutions is facilitated by entering into discussions with a collaborative mindset instead of an aggressive one. Behaving with dignity, compassion, and an open mind to comprehend the supplier's point of view helps build rapport and create a positive atmosphere for constructive dialogues.

Concentrating on the value offer rather than just the price is a vital negotiating tactic. Showcasing the advantages of a long-term collaboration, such as steady orders, the possibility of higher volumes, and shared objectives, might encourage the supplier to agree to more advantageous conditions. The emphasis can be shifted from cost-cutting to value creation by highlighting shared benefits and illustrating how the partnership can benefit both sides.

Skilled negotiators also make use of the knowledge asymmetry power. Businesses can improve their bargaining position by obtaining and evaluating information on market trends, possible substitutes, and the supplier's rivals. This information available during negotiations might show that the company is ready, knowledgeable, and willing to look into other solutions if needed.

Comprehending the mechanics of timing is an additional crucial tactic. Securing advantageous terms can be increased by negotiating at the correct moment, such as near the end of a financial quarter or during a supplier's period of low demand. During slow times, suppliers could be more amenable to haggling to reach their sales goals or keep steady production levels.

In negotiations, the skill of yielding is equally essential. Skilled negotiators understand when to give in and when to maintain their position. Prioritizing concessions that are less expensive or crucial to the company is vital. Still, it's also essential to make sure that significant progress is made in more critical areas. Concessions are a helpful negotiation strategy for a fair settlement that pleases both sides.

Understanding and creating contracts and agreements is essential to formalizing the arrangement once the details have been discussed. A well-written contract establishes each party's obligations, rights, and expectations and gives the commercial relationship a defined structure. It is crucial to ensure the contract covers every critical detail, including payment terms, delivery dates, quality requirements, pricing, confidentiality, and dispute resolution procedures.

The scope of work outlines the goods or services to be rendered, and the performance metrics, which set the parameters for quality and delivery, are essential components of a contract. The payment conditions, including the amount, mode, and date, must be made explicit. The company can avoid financial risks by implementing late fees and penalties provisions.

Delivery terms should specify the deadlines, shipping obligations, and loss risk. Clarifying the logistics and obligations associated with the shipping of commodities can be achieved by selecting the Incoterms (International Commercial Terms). Quality assurance clauses should outline the accepted standards and processes for inspections, refunds, and replacements.

To safeguard confidential corporate information and intellectual property, confidentiality agreements are essential. Non-disclosure agreements (NDAs) can protect intellectual information from being used or distributed without contract authorization.

To handle possible issues that may develop throughout the contract's execution, dispute resolution procedures are crucial. Effective conflict management can be aided by defining the arbitration, mediation, litigation procedures, and jurisdiction for any court cases.

Settling terms and prices with suppliers necessitates a calculated strategy that balances short-term financial advantages and long-term relationship development. Thorough planning, precise goal-setting, rapport-building, value-focused talks, taking advantage of knowledge asymmetry, time awareness, and calculated concessions are all examples of effective negotiation tactics. Comprehending and crafting detailed contracts and agreements serves to codify the agreed-upon terms, provide a well-defined structure for the business partnership, and protect each party's interests. Gaining proficiency in these areas can help companies improve profitability, streamline their supply chains, and establish enduring relationships with their suppliers.

CHAPTER IV

Setting Up Your Online Store

Choosing the Right E-commerce Platform

Opening an online store is an essential first step for companies trying to reach a wider audience and boost revenue. Selecting the appropriate platform is critical to any successful e-commerce endeavor since it dramatically impacts the store's functionality, scalability, and overall user experience. Businesses may make an informed decision by being aware of the capabilities and benefits that platforms like BigCommerce, WooCommerce, and Shopify offer.

Selecting the best e-commerce platform requires weighing several important factors corresponding to your company's objectives and needs. Among the most well-liked choices are Shopify, WooCommerce, and BigCommerce, each with unique advantages.

Prominent e-commerce platform Shopify is renowned for its feature-rich features and user-friendliness. Since Shopify offers a wholly hosted solution, business owners can concentrate on their core competencies while they let them handle technical responsibilities like server management and security. Shopify's user-friendly interface makes it accessible to those with little technical understanding, which is one of its key advantages. Setting up a store is simple because of the drag-and-drop builder and the abundance of configurable themes.

Along with a wide range of capabilities, Shopify also provides marketing tools, inventory management, and safe payment gateways. With the help of the many connectors and add-ons available in its App Store, companies can improve the functionality of their stores. Shopify lets businesses reach a wider audience by supporting a variety of sales channels, such as social media and online marketplaces like Amazon. However, it works on a subscription basis, and if you choose not to use Shopify Payments, there can be extra transaction costs. Because of the potential cost increase, firms must carefully assess their budget.

Conversely, WooCommerce is a WordPress plugin that turns a WordPress website into an e-commerce store with all the features needed. Because it is an open-source platform, companies with specialized demands and technical know-how can benefit significantly from its flexibility and customization choices. While WooCommerce is free, companies must pay for domain registration, hosting, and additional premium themes or plugins.

WooCommerce's versatility is one of its main advantages. It can be significantly altered from functionality to design to satisfy specific corporate needs. This platform offers an extensive library of plugins to increase its functionality and support for many payment gateways and shipping methods. Additionally, SEO-friendly, WooCommerce helps companies raise their search engine ranks and draw in natural traffic. However, since it's a self-hosted solution, companies must handle technical issues like security, backups, and updates, which may require hiring a developer or acquiring more technical expertise.

BigCommerce is an additional robust platform that blends some of the functionality of WooCommerce with the simplicity of Shopify. It is a fully hosted solution that offers online retailers a dependable and safe environment. BigCommerce is a good option for companies aiming to expand dramatically because of its reputation for scalability. It has many integrated features, such as sophisticated SEO tools, multi-channel sales, and robust analytics.

BigCommerce's lack of transaction fees might be a significant advantage for high-volume sellers. Due to its broad integration features may be easily connected to a wide range of third-party services and apps. Additionally, BigCommerce provides top-notch customer service, guaranteeing that companies may acquire assistance when required. But compared to Shopify, the platform could be more challenging and have a higher learning curve because of its extensive feature set.

Several elements must be considered to ensure the e-commerce platform fits the company's needs. It must be easy to use, especially for non-technical people. The time and effort needed to set up and run the store can be significantly decreased with a platform that offers extensive assistance and an easy-to-use interface.

Scalability is still another essential element. The platform should be able to manage more transactions, inventory, and traffic as the company expands without sacrificing functionality. This involves considering the platform's ability to interface with additional tools and systems that might be needed as the company grows.

Options for payment gateways are essential since they impact the shopping experience of the customer. The platform should support Multiple payment methods so that users can select their favorite one. Furthermore, the confidentiality of these transactions is crucial, requiring strong security measures to safeguard private client information.

Businesses can develop a distinctive brand identity and customize the purchasing experience for their clients by utilizing customization possibilities. Companies can tailor their stores to suit specific requirements and tastes using platforms with many themes, plugins, and integrations.

Increasing traffic to the online store requires marketing tools and SEO. Features that allow email marketing, social media integration, and search engine optimization can improve visibility and draw in more visitors.

Lastly, expenditures to be considered include transaction fees, fees for extra features, and possible expenses for technical support or development, in addition to the platform's subscription fees or one-time costs.

In conclusion, the e-commerce platform must be carefully considered before launching an online store. BigCommerce, WooCommerce, and Shopify all provide special features and advantages that meet various business requirements. Businesses can select the best platform to support their growth and success in the cutthroat online marketplace by weighing factors like pricing, SEO and marketing tools, payment alternatives, payment simplicity, and customization capabilities.

Designing Your Store

More than just showing products is involved in the multifaceted process of designing an online store. To build a shopping environment that is both efficient and interesting, significant consideration must be given to branding, graphic design, user experience (UX), and navigation. In addition to drawing clients, a well-designed online store stimulates them to browse, interact, and eventually make a buy.

An online store's essential components, branding, and visual design, assist create a distinct identity and set the company apart from rivals. Effective branding is critical to developing a distinctive and consistent image that appeals to the target market. This includes using images, typography, color schemes, and logos that express the character and values of the brand. A colorful children's brand might use vibrant colors, fun typefaces, and whimsical images to generate a sense of joy and excitement. In contrast, a luxury business might use elegant fonts, high-quality photographs, and a sophisticated color palette to indicate exclusivity and premium quality.

Beyond just being beautiful, visual design is essential to creating the ideal user experience. A simple, eye-catching layout can improve the site's usability and significantly impact users' buying choices. Features that aid in greater product understanding and decision-making include crisp photos, product videos, and thorough explanations. Consistent visual components, such as buttons, banners, and icons, improve the store's overall professionalism and coherence.

In the design of an online store, navigation, and user experience are equally important. UX is concerned with how a website feels overall and how simple it is for users to interact with. Customer satisfaction may be raised, and friction points can significantly decrease with a smooth and straightforward user experience. Since a large percentage of online shopping is done on mobile devices, the first step is ensuring the website is responsive and mobile-friendly. The arrangement should adjust to various screen dimensions while preserving its visual appeal and usability on all gadgets.

A crucial element of user experience (UX) is navigation, which leads users across the website and facilitates their rapid and effective search for what they're looking for. Clear categories, subcategories, and filters that enable users to focus their search according to particular parameters like cost, size, color, and brand are all part of a well-designed navigation system. Each section's content should be indicated by the intuitive labels on the main navigation menu prominently displayed. A search bar is a must-have for clients who know exactly what they want because it allows them to find products immediately without browsing through categories.

Since the homepage frequently serves as a customer's initial point of contact, it is an essential component of store design. It should display highlighted goods, special offers, and essential company messaging attractively and educationally. Marked calls to action (CTAs), like "Shop Now" or "Learn More," direct shoppers to the next phase of their purchasing process. Visual hierarchy plays a crucial role in drawing attention to the most essential parts by using size, color, and location to emphasize the most significant regions.

Any online store's centerpiece is its product page, and its design may make or break a sale. Comprehensive information on every product page should include clear photos taken from various perspectives, thorough descriptions, specifications, client testimonials, and prices. The "Add to Cart" button should be noticeable and straightforward to locate. Suggestions or related products can boost sales and enhance the buying experience.

Another essential part of UX is the checkout process. Ensuring a seamless and uncomplicated checkout experience is crucial since an intricate or protracted checkout procedure may result in cart abandonment.

Encouraging guests to check out, offering several payment methods, and reducing the steps needed can all improve the customer experience. Customers are guided through the process and reassured that their order is being handled with clear instructions, progress indicators, and confirmation messages.

Adding personalized components can also improve the purchasing experience. Customers can feel appreciated and understood by accessing features like targeted promotions, customized email marketing, and product suggestions based on browsing history. By making the purchasing experience more relevant and exciting, personalization increases the chance of returning customers and repeat purchases.

Apart from these components, it's imperative to guarantee rapid loading speeds and robust security protocols. Strong security measures safeguard essential consumer information and foster confidence, yet slow-loading websites can irritate visitors and increase bounce rates.

To sum up, creating an online store requires striking a precise balance between user experience, navigation, branding, and visual design. Good visual design and branding establish a distinctive and appealing identity, and smooth user navigation and experience make it simple for customers to locate and buy things. Businesses may build an online store that draws visitors and turns them into devoted clients by concentrating on these factors, eventually leading to long-term success in the cutthroat world of e-commerce.

Product Listings and Descriptions

E-commerce relies heavily on the creation of compelling product listings and descriptions, which have the power to influence a customer's choice to buy. In addition to educating potential customers about the products, well-written descriptions and excellent photos help pique their interest, foster trust, and increase conversion rates.

Knowing your target market is the first step in creating compelling product descriptions. You may adjust the language, tone, and content by identifying your target audience to suit their interests and requirements. For example, a lifestyle-oriented audience may be more interested in a product's advantages and visual attractiveness, but a technical audience may value thorough specifications and data.

A good product description should be thorough but brief, giving the reader all the information they need without going overboard. A compelling headline summarizing the product should come first, followed by a short synopsis emphasizing its salient characteristics and advantages. This summary should address the primary query that every prospective customer has: "Why should I buy this product?"
More precise information should be covered in the description's body. It emphasizes the distinctive characteristics of a product, including its materials, dimensions, and capabilities, and aids in customers' understanding of what makes it unique. It's critical to convert these features into advantages by describing how they will improve the customer's quality of life or address a specific issue. For instance, elucidate how a jacket's waterproof material keeps the wearer dry and comfortable during inclement weather rather than asserting that it does.

Product descriptions can be more interesting by adding a storytelling aspect, features, and benefits. Customers can feel more emotionally connected to a product when the development process, inspiration, and ethical production methods are shared. Using a narrative approach makes the description more engaging and helps the product fit the buyer's values and goals.

Adding rich imagery and sensory language to product descriptions can also improve them. Customers can better mentally see and experience the goods when descriptive language appeals to their senses. Saying "rich, full-bodied flavor with notes of chocolate and a smooth finish" paints a far more attractive picture of a coffee mix than just saying it's "good coffee."

Another critical component of creating compelling product descriptions is SEO (Search Engine Optimization). Enhancing the product's search engine exposure can be achieved by utilizing pertinent keywords that prospective consumers will likely enter. However, to keep the description appealing and readable, it's crucial to use these keywords organically.

It's crucial to pair strong product descriptions with excellent photos. Pictures give consumers a clear picture of the product, enabling them to see exactly what they are buying. Clear, well-lit, high-resolution images can significantly impact drawing in and holding onto customers' attention.

A complete product view is provided via numerous photos taken from various perspectives. When it comes to apparel, for example, providing buyers with close-ups of details like stitching and fabric texture in addition to the front, back, and side views all aid in their decision-making. Including photos for each variety of a product—such as different colors or sizes—ensures that customers know exactly what to expect.

Lifestyle photos that feature the product in use or an authentic setting have the potential to be more effective. They might highlight useful features or visual appeal and assist clients in seeing how the product fits into their lives. For instance, a lifestyle photo of a sofa in a tastefully furnished living room may persuade viewers more than a straightforward product photo against a white backdrop.

Furthermore, photos should be optimized for quick loading times without sacrificing quality. Images that load slowly can annoy visitors and increase their bounce rate. To balance loading speed and quality, use formats like PNG for images with transparent backgrounds and JPEG for photos.

Product listings can be improved even further by adding videos. An enhanced and more engaging experience can be had by watching videos that show the product being used, describing its characteristics, or showcasing an unboxing. They can respond to frequently asked queries or worries, demonstrate the practical advantages of the product, and foster audience trust.

Including client endorsements and reviews with product details and photos can help establish trust and sway consumers' decisions. Genuine user reviews act as social proof, convincing prospective purchasers of the product's dependability and quality.

In conclusion, skillfully written language and excellent images create successful product listings and descriptions. Product descriptions should be written with the intended reader in mind, emphasizing features and benefits while drawing the reader in with sensory language and storytelling. Superior photographs offer a visual depiction of the goods, presenting various angles and authentic context to assist buyers in making well-informed choices. By putting these components together, companies can create product listings that draw customers in, foster credibility, and encourage conversions—all of which improve the overall shopping experience and increase revenue.

Setting Up Payment Gateways

Installing payment gateways is an essential first step in starting an online store because it directly impacts the checkout process and the customer's perception of the company. Payment gateways guarantee the security of transactions while facilitating money flow from consumers to retailers. For a purchasing experience to be seamless and reliable, the correct payment methods and robust security measures must be used.

The most widely used payment methods differ based on the area, clientele, and commercial requirements. Payment gateways like PayPal, Stripe, and Square and conventional credit card processors like Visa and MasterCard are among the most often used. These choices are all appropriate for various kinds of organizations because they each have unique characteristics and advantages.

One of the most well-known and reliable online payment processors is PayPal. Customers can use a credit card, bank account, or PayPal balance to make payments. One of its main benefits is that PayPal is widely accepted and simple to use for both customers and businesses. It provides a simplified checkout procedure that may lower cart abandonment rates. Furthermore, PayPal offers robust policies for protecting buyers and sellers, boosting security and confidence.

Another well-liked payment gateway is Stripe, well-known for its developer-friendly API that enables companies to customize their payment procedures extensively. Credit cards, ACH transfers, and digital wallets like Apple Pay and Google Pay are just a few payment options that Stripe accepts. Recurring billing, subscription management, and multi-currency compatibility are just a few of its many features. Businesses wishing to provide a safe and adaptable payment solution can rely on Stripe because of its sophisticated security features and fraud detection capabilities.

Although its point-of-sale systems are its primary focus, Square also provides extensive online payment options. The payment gateway offered by Square is easy to use and works well with all of its other services, including inventory management and invoicing. Numerous payment options, such as digital wallets and credit cards, are supported. Square is desirable for small and medium-sized enterprises due to its clear pricing structure, lack of additional costs, and strong security measures.

Because they are well-known and widely accepted, traditional credit card processors like Visa and MasterCard continue to be in demand. Since they serve many customers, these payment options are crucial for every online business. Working with a merchant account provider and a payment gateway service, which facilitates the transaction process, is usually necessary to integrate credit card payments.

It is crucial to provide security and confidence in payment processing. When making purchases online, customers need to know that their private information is secure. Using technologies such as Secure Socket Layer (SSL) certificates, which encrypt data passed between the customer's browser and the merchant's server, is part of implementing strong security measures. Sensitive data, including credit card numbers and personal information, is protected by this encryption, which also helps prevent unwanted access.

Another essential component of guaranteeing payment security is adhering to the Payment Card Industry Data Security Standard (PCI DSS). A collection of security guidelines called PCI DSS is intended to safeguard cardholder data during and after a financial transaction. To prevent fraud and data breaches, businesses that handle, store, or transfer credit card information must abide by these rules. Upholding a secure network, safeguarding cardholder data, putting robust access control mechanisms in place, and routinely testing and monitoring networks are all part of compliance.

An additional layer of security for payment data is provided by tokenization. Sensitive data, including credit card numbers, are replaced by a one-of-a-kind token or unique identification that is only usable within the particular transaction environment. This procedure ensures that cybercriminals cannot use data for anything, even if data is intercepted.

Security measures for payment gateways also need fraud detection and prevention technologies. Numerous payment processors, like PayPal and Stripe, have sophisticated fraud detection algorithms that examine transactions instantly to spot possibly fraudulent activity. Using large datasets and machine learning methods, these systems look for trends and abnormalities that can point to fraud. By implementing such measures, businesses can reduce the risk of chargebacks and fraudulent transactions.

Two-factor authentication (2FA) is an additional security technique that works well. Asking users to confirm their identity using a second factor—such as a code texted to their mobile device—in addition to their password it provides an extra degree of protection. Even if login credentials are compromised, this helps prevent unwanted access to client accounts.

Customer trust can be increased by communicating security measures openly and understandably. Customers are reassured that their data is handled safely when security badges, such as SSL certifications and PCI compliance logos, are displayed on the checkout page. Another way to foster trust is to be transparent about privacy rules and data protection procedures.

In summary, to establish trust and security, a payment gateway setup requires deciding on well-liked and dependable payment methods and putting strong security measures in place. Traditional credit card processors, Square, PayPal, and Stripe all have unique benefits and meet various demands of businesses. Protecting consumer data and fostering trust requires ensuring the security of financial transactions via SSL certificates, PCI DSS compliance, tokenization, fraud detection technologies, and two-factor authentication. Businesses may build a safe and easy payment process by concentrating on these components, eventually increasing client happiness and loyalty.

CHAPTER V

Inventory and Order Management

Managing Inventory Without Holding Stock

Managing orders and inventory is essential to operating a profitable e-commerce company. Dropshipping, or inventory management without retaining goods, has become a business strategy for numerous companies. This strategy for efficient inventory management depends on utilizing suppliers' inventory and incorporating cutting-edge technologies. Dropshipping can help reduce the operational and financial risks of keeping physical inventory.

Working closely with suppliers who handle the inventory on the retailer's behalf is essential to inventory management without keeping stock. Under this arrangement, the supplier manages storage, packaging, and customer-direct shipment while the retailer markets and sells the goods. This configuration minimizes expenses and lowers the possibility of overstocking or understocking by enabling firms to provide a large selection of products without making an upfront inventory investment.

The low entry barrier is one of dropshipping's main benefits. Retailers can launch their businesses with less initial cost because they are not required to buy merchandise in advance. Because of this, drop shipping is a desirable choice for company owners and small enterprises wishing to branch out into the online retail space. Furthermore, shops can test new products and react fast to market trends because they may provide a wide choice of products without making a significant financial commitment.

Choosing trustworthy suppliers who can deliver dependable delivery services and high-quality products is necessary while using their inventory. A dropshipping company's ability to complete orders primarily rests on the supplier's ability to do it quickly and precisely. Consequently, conducting in-depth research and screening possible vendors is essential. Retailers want to seek suppliers with a track record of success, glowing testimonials, and effective contact routes. Establishing guidelines for quality assurance, return procedures, and shipment schedules promotes customer satisfaction and a seamless working environment.

To effectively manage inventories and orders, suppliers must be collaborated with and communicated with. To prevent selling out-of-stock items, retailers want real-time access to the inventory levels of their suppliers. Strong integration between the supplier's inventory management system and the retailer's e-commerce platform is necessary for this. Modern hardware and software enable this integration and guarantee smooth operations.

Retailers may efficiently manage their dropshipping business with several inventory management systems. These technologies offer features like order processing, inventory tracking, and real-time stock-level updates. An inventory management system (IMS) is one tool merchants can use to manage product listings, keep track of orders from various suppliers, and monitor stock levels. Many inventory management tasks can be automated by an IMS, which reduces human error and saves time.

Another crucial tool is a dropshipping automation program that interfaces with the supplier's systems and the retailer's e-commerce platform. This software automates Order fulfillment, which updates consumers on shipment status and routes orders to suppliers. Retailers can concentrate on marketing and customer service instead of the intricacies of order management by automating these operations.

Several apps and plugins on platforms like Shopify, WooCommerce, and BigCommerce are made especially for dropshipping companies. Through these interfaces, businesses can expedite order processing, synchronize their online shop with suppliers' inventories, and receive real-time updates on product availability. For example, two well-known solutions that make dropshipping easier are Oberlo, a Shopify app, and AliDropship, a WooCommerce plugin. These tools connect retailers with suppliers, manage inventory, and automate order fulfillment.

Keeping product information current and correct is another essential inventory management component without storing stock. To avoid errors and unhappy customers, retailers must ensure that product descriptions, prices, and photos match the supplier's inventory. The retailer's and supplier's systems must regularly synchronize for this to happen. Automated tools and APIs (Application Programming Interfaces) can help with this.

A satisfying client experience depends on efficient order management. Orders must be immediately notified to the supplier to be fulfilled after they are placed. This includes creating purchase orders, verifying stock availability, and monitoring the status of shipments. These responsibilities can be effectively handled by advanced order management systems (OMS), which can also guarantee on-time delivery to customers and give retailers information on the progress of each order.

Setting up precise procedures and guidelines for managing different situations, such as stockouts or refunds, is crucial in addition to automated technologies. Establishing protocols for handling such circumstances in close collaboration with suppliers will help retailers keep consumers informed and satisfied all along the way.

Demand planning and inventory forecasting are crucial for running a dropshipping company. Retailers still need to predict client demand even though they don't physically hold goods to prevent stockouts and guarantee product availability. Inventory forecasting systems assist suppliers and retailers in aligning their operations and maintaining ideal stock levels by utilizing past sales data and industry trends to forecast future demand.

In summary, utilizing suppliers' inventory and cutting-edge technologies for efficient inventory and order administration is critical to managing inventory without retaining stock. Many advantages come with dropshipping, such as decreased operating expenses, a more extensive product selection, and less financial risk. On the other hand, this model's success hinges on integrating robust inventory management technologies, choosing trustworthy suppliers, and keeping lines of communication open. Retailers may improve consumer satisfaction, streamline operations, and establish a profitable e-commerce firm by implementing these tactics and technologies.

Order Fulfillment Process

The order fulfillment process, which includes all the procedures involved in receiving, processing, and delivering customer orders, is essential to e-commerce operations. To guarantee a smooth and practical experience, several coordinated actions are needed from when a customer puts an order to the point of delivery. Suppliers must be carefully collaborated with to complete orders and deliver goods to clients throughout this process.

ORDER FULFILLMENT

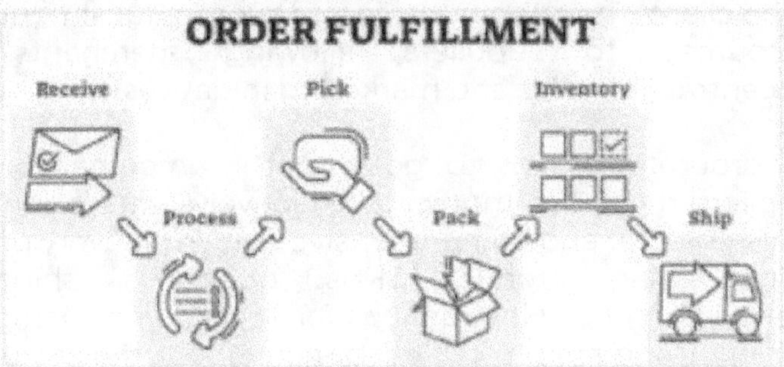

The order fulfillment procedure usually starts when a customer orders via the retailer's website or another sales channel. Orders must be processed quickly upon receipt to begin the fulfillment process. Verifying the order's data, such as the products requested, the quantities, the shipping address, and any specific instructions the buyer may have given, is part of this process. Many of these operations are automated by order processing software or systems, which speeds up the process and lowers manual mistake rates.

Transaction fulfillment involves selecting, packaging, and shipping the products to the consumer after processing the transaction. This entails removing the products from the warehouse, securely packing them, and making shipment or delivery arrangements in a typical fulfillment model where the retailer keeps its inventory. On the other hand, with a dropshipping model, the supplier manages the fulfillment process, and the merchant does not maintain stock.

Muscular coordination and communication are necessary when working with suppliers to fulfill orders when using a dropshipping model. The supplier receives the order data from the store as soon as it is received, along with any special requirements or instructions. After selecting the items from their stock, the supplier packages them according to the retailer's requirements and sends them to the client. The operational facets of order fulfillment are outsourced to suppliers, allowing merchants to concentrate on sales and marketing initiatives.

For order fulfillment to go smoothly, merchants and suppliers must communicate effectively. Retailers must furnish precise and comprehensive details on every order, encompassing product SKUs, quantities, shipping addresses, and any instructions for special treatment. For retailers to be able to tell customers about the status of their purchases, suppliers must reply to them with order status updates, shipping confirmations, and tracking details.

Maintaining openness and visibility into the fulfillment process is essential for merchants and customers. To trace the development of each order and handle any potential problems, retailers require real-time access to order status and tracking data. A robust integration between the supplier's systems and the retailer's e-commerce platform is needed to enable smooth communication and data sharing.

Delivery to the customer is the last stage of the fulfillment process once the order is dispatched. Coordinating with logistics companies or shipping carriers is required for precise and on-time delivery. Giving clients access to tracking details enables them to keep an eye on the status of their shipments and predict when they will arrive. Keeping customers informed about delivery schedules, shipping charges, and any possible delays lowers the risk of unhappiness and helps control customer expectations.

The order fulfillment process may include extra duties like inventory management, returns processing, customer service, and the essential phases of order processing, fulfillment, and delivery. A positive and seamless shopping experience depends on efficiently administrating these duties.

In addition to preventing stockouts and overstocking, inventory management guarantees that products are available for fulfillment. To ensure that merchandise is accessible at the time of customer orders, retailers must keep precise inventory records and keep an eye on stock levels. Process disruptions can be avoided by closely collaborating with suppliers to synchronize inventory levels and refill stock as needed.

An additional crucial component of order fulfillment is handling returns. Customers can return products for several reasons, including flaws, damages, or just a simple change of heart. Retailers must have well-defined rules and processes for managing returns, including quick and effective replacements or refunds. Refunds can lessen overall profitability by collaborating with suppliers to expedite the processing of returns and reduce the cost of return shipping.

To fulfill orders, customer service is essential because it helps fix problems that could arise before, during, or after the sale. This includes responding to customer questions, settling disagreements over orders, and handling grievances or issues. Staff members must be competent, responsive, and accommodating to give consumers fast and helpful service.

In summary, retailers and suppliers work closely to execute a sequence of coordinated processes from order placement to delivery as part of the order fulfillment process. In a dropshipping model, where suppliers manage the operational parts of order fulfillment, working with them is crucial. Good communication, transparency, and visibility into the fulfillment process are essential for a seamless and satisfying purchasing experience. Merchants may boost business growth, increase customer satisfaction, and improve operational efficiency by optimizing the order fulfillment process and close collaboration with suppliers.

Handling Returns and Refunds

Refunds and returns handling is a crucial component of e-commerce operations that must be carefully planned and carried out to guarantee customer happiness and preserve profitability. Having a transparent return policy and effectively handling returns is critical to giving customers a satisfying shopping experience and earning their trust.

The first step in developing a straightforward returns policy is creating clear, user-friendly product returns rules. A transparent returns policy outlines the terms and conditions under which customers can return things. These conditions include the return period, acceptable reasons, and any associated costs or restrictions. Customers' expectations can be set, and the retailer can decrease misunderstandings by clearly communicating this policy on their website.

A successful returns policy should not only serve the requirements of customers but also defend the retailer's interests. While retailers may impose certain conditions, such as requiring items to be returned in their original condition or within a specified time period, it's crucial to be flexible and accommodating to customers' needs. By providing options like shop credit, refunds, exchanges, and replacement products, retailers can show their commitment to customer satisfaction, which is the cornerstone of successful e-commerce operations.

Establishing streamlined procedures and guidelines for managing returns from start to finish is necessary for efficient return management. This entails giving clients precise information on how to start a return, whether via a phone call, email, or web portal and ensuring that return requests are promptly acknowledged and confirmed. Automated methods or software can make this procedure more efficient and less labor-intensive.

Retailers must evaluate a return request's integrity and choose the best action after receiving one. This could entail reviewing the returned item to ensure it satisfies the requirements listed in the returns policy, like being in its original packing, unused, and undamaged. Having a specialized group or department in charge of returns helps speed up the procedure and guarantee consistency in the choices made.

Retailers must expeditiously process the refund or exchange once the return is accepted. This involves issuing refunds to the customer's original payment method, providing store credit, or arranging for a replacement product to be shipped. Maintaining openness and fostering confidence is facilitated by keeping in touch with customers at every stage of the return process. This includes verifying receipt of the returned item, handling refunds, and giving information on the progress of swaps or replacements.

Recording and analyzing return data is not just a task, but a powerful tool for continuous improvement in e-commerce operations. By tracking metrics like return rates, returns' causes, and customer comments, retailers can gain valuable insights into areas where items or procedures might need to be modified. For instance, high return rates for specific products could be a sign of poor quality or mismatches between what customers want and what the product is described as. By proactively addressing these issues, retailers can reduce returns, increase customer happiness, and pave the way for long-term success.

Retailers must be ready to handle supplier or manufacturer returns in addition to customer-initiated returns for various reasons, including overstocking, product selection changes, or defective or broken merchandise. Implementing well-defined protocols for managing supplier returns, encompassing communication avenues, paperwork prerequisites, and resolution schedules, facilitates prompt and effective resolution while mitigating operational disturbances.

Effective communication with suppliers is not just a task, but a key to successful returns management in e-commerce operations. By building solid partnerships with suppliers through openness, cooperation, and trust, retailers can make returns processing easier and proactively handle problems. Frequent communication, such as performance reviews and feedback sessions, not only helps to maintain alignment on return policies and processes but also strengthens these connections, fostering a sense of collaboration and shared responsibility in the audience.

In summary, managing refunds and returns is a crucial component of e-commerce operations that calls for thorough preparation, precise guidelines, and effective procedures. A clear returns policy that balances the consumer's needs and the retailer's interests is crucial to fostering trust and offering a satisfying shopping experience. Establishing streamlined procedures, having good communication with suppliers and consumers, and evaluating return data to find areas for improvement are all necessary for managing returns successfully. In the highly competitive world of e-commerce, businesses may successfully handle returns and refunds while preserving profitability and fostering long-term success by prioritizing customer pleasure and operational effectiveness.

Automation Tools

Automation technologies are not just a trend but a necessity in the modern business landscape, particularly in dropshipping. These tools are not just about simplifying procedures but boosting productivity and providing benefits that can significantly impact a drop shipping company's growth and success. Understanding these specific advantages and the role of automation in drop shipping is critical to optimizing operations and achieving sustainable development.

Drop shipping stands out as a business model that enables businesses to sell things without retaining inventory in the fiercely competitive and fast-paced world of e-commerce. Instead, the merchant buys the item from a third-party supplier upon receiving an order from the buyer, who ships it straight to the customer. This approach lowers the expenses and hazards related to stock maintenance. Still, it also comes with particular difficulties, like managing supplier relationships, ensuring orders are filled on time, and maintaining inventory levels. These issues are addressed by automation solutions, which decrease errors, automate tedious operations, and give business owners more time to concentrate on client happiness and expansion.

A significant advantage of automation in drop shipping is increased operational effectiveness. Manual activities, such as order processing, inventory management, and customer support, can be time-consuming and prone to errors. Automation tools make these operations more efficient and guarantee they are finished on time and correctly. For instance, an automated system can produce tracking information for the consumer, update inventory levels, and give the supplier order data as soon as an order is placed on an e-commerce site. This reduces the possibility of human error and expedites the fulfillment process, increasing customer satisfaction and lowering the number of post-sale problems.

Another crucial area where automation is quite helpful is inventory management. It can be challenging to keep track of stock levels across several vendors, mainly as a business grows. Real-time inventory data synchronization is possible with automation technologies, guaranteeing that the e-commerce platform always shows available stock. This avoids overselling, which raises the risk of unhappy customers and higher return rates. Additionally, automated inventory alerts can tell business owners when stock levels are low, allowing them to replenish products proactively and avoid stockouts.

One of the most significant areas where automation can make a difference is customer service, a crucial aspect of any e-commerce operation. Automated customer care technologies, such as chatbots and AI-powered support systems, can handle common queries and issues 24/7, providing immediate customer assistance. This eliminates the need for customers to wait for human interaction and ensures they receive prompt responses, enhancing their overall experience. Furthermore, automation frees up customer support agents to focus on more complex issues, improving the quality of service provided.

Automation in drop shipping is also very beneficial to marketing and sales initiatives. For example, automated email marketing campaigns can re-engage customers, nurture leads, and push products without requiring regular user input. The success of these advertisements can be increased by tailoring them to the preferences and behavior of the target audience. Automation technologies can also be used to track the effectiveness of ads, manage social media posts, and analyze customer data to improve marketing strategy. With this data-driven strategy, marketing initiatives are efficient and well-targeted, optimizing return on investment.

The scalability of a drop shipping firm is another area where automation has a considerable influence. It becomes unfeasible to manually handle growing order volumes, inventory, and customer interactions as the business expands. Automation solutions can easily handle large-scale operations, enabling organizations to grow without sacrificing productivity or customer care. This scalability guarantees sustainable growth and the ability of the company to satisfy growing customer demands.

Through automation, drop shipping financial administration is also made more accessible. Real-time tracking of sales, costs, and profits via automated accounting software gives company owners a precise and understandable financial picture. This reduces manual bookkeeping time, and economic data is always current and prepared for analysis. To move the company forward, automated financial reporting can be used to spot trends, control cash flow, and make wise decisions.

Moreover, automation solutions boost supplier management by providing capabilities such as automated order routing and supplier performance tracking. These solutions ensure that orders are automatically forwarded to the correct supplier depending on predetermined parameters like location, price, and stock levels. Business owners may use performance tracking features to monitor product quality, delivery schedules, and supplier dependability. This information helps them choose which suppliers to work with based on data analysis.

Conclusively, incorporating automation technologies in drop shipping presents many advantages that optimize processes, augment effectiveness, and facilitate expandable expansion. These technologies allow business owners to focus on strategic operations like marketing and client engagement by automating time-consuming and repetitive processes. Automation benefits the drop-shipping model in many ways, including better inventory control, robust customer service, effective marketing, and sound financial management. Leveraging automation will be essential for firms hoping to stay competitive and succeed over the long run as e-commerce develops.

CHAPTER VI

Marketing and Driving Traffic

Introduction to E-commerce Marketing

The dynamic and multidimensional discipline of e-commerce marketing is essential to online businesses since it drives traffic and generates sales. Understanding the many marketing channels and the significance of a well-crafted marketing plan becomes vital for e-commerce success as the digital world grows. This e-commerce marketing introduction highlights the importance of a strategic approach in accomplishing corporate objectives and summarizes essential marketing channels.

Fundamentally, e-commerce marketing refers to all strategies and actions used to advertise goods and services online and draw prospective clients to an e-commerce platform. The main objectives are increasing visibility, generating traffic, and converting visitors into paying clients. Leveraging numerous marketing channels is essential to reaching a broad audience and optimizing sales potential, especially in the competitive e-commerce industry.

Search engine optimization is one of the most well-known e-commerce marketing platforms (SEO). To raise a website's position on search engine results pages (SERPs), SEO entails improving the website's content, structure, and technological elements. A higher ranking raises the possibility of drawing in organic traffic from customers looking for related goods or services. Researching keywords, optimizing pages for search engines, producing content of the highest caliber, and constructing reliable backlinks are all effective SEO techniques. By increasing their search engine visibility, E-commerce companies can improve their online presence and attract more qualified leads.

Another effective tool for e-commerce companies to increase targeted visitors to their websites is pay-per-click (PPC) advertising. PPC advertising, like Google Ads and Bing Ads, entails bidding on keywords associated with the provided goods and services. Advertising is a cost-effective approach to draw in potential clients because advertisers pay a price each time their ad is clicked. PPC campaigns ensure that the most relevant audience sees the advertising by allowing extreme targeting based on user behavior, location, and demographics. Furthermore, PPC offers instant awareness and can yield results quickly, which makes it an excellent choice for increasing traffic and sales during promotional times.

E-commerce marketing tactics are only complete with social media marketing. Social media sites like Facebook, Instagram, Twitter, and Pinterest present distinctive chances to interact with prospective clients and increase brand recognition. Social media allows businesses to produce and distribute information, carry out focused advertising efforts, and have real-time conversations with their audience. Influencers with sizable followings are used in influencer marketing to pitch things to their audience. E-commerce companies can reach new markets and gain the trust of potential clients by working with influencers. Long-term success also depends on community building and customer loyalty, fostered by social media's interactive nature.

Email marketing is still one of the best ways to increase e-commerce traffic and sales. Businesses can communicate with their audience in a targeted and personalized manner by gathering email addresses from customers and website users. Email marketing can be used to offer deals, introduce new items, nurture leads, and offer insightful material. Automated email sequences, like post-purchase follow-ups, abandoned cart alerts, and welcome series, guarantee that companies maintain contact with their clients during purchasing. Email marketing is essential to any e-commerce marketing plan because of its high return on investment (ROI).

Another crucial channel is content marketing, which concentrates on producing and disseminating worthwhile, timely, consistent material to draw in and hold on to a target audience. Content marketing can take many forms for e-commerce enterprises, such as blog articles, videos, infographics, and tutorials. In addition to building authority and trust, excellent content uses SEO to increase organic traffic. Potential buyers can be helped by content marketing, which can also solve their problems, inform them about the advantages of products, and help them through the purchasing process. E-commerce companies can cultivate brand loyalty and long-lasting relationships with their audience by providing valuable content.

Businesses use affiliate marketing as a performance-based channel to pay affiliates for bringing customers and traffic to their websites. Affiliates market products via their websites, blogs, and social media accounts. They also get paid a commission for every sale made due to their referral links. Through this channel, e-commerce companies can reach a wider audience and leverage the affiliate's audience at no expense to them up front. Businesses can expand their consumer base and boost their credibility by collaborating with reliable affiliates.

In e-commerce, the value of a carefully thought-out marketing plan cannot be emphasized through identifying target audiences, goal-setting, and describing strategies and channels to be employed; a marketing strategy offers a road map for accomplishing company objectives. By ensuring that all marketing initiatives are coordinated and coherent, it maximizes their effectiveness. E-commerce companies need a strategic plan to save money on fragmented or inefficient marketing initiatives.

Businesses can assess and evaluate the effectiveness of their marketing initiatives with the help of a thorough marketing plan. Companies can learn what works and doesn't by establishing key performance indicators (KPIs) and monitoring data like traffic, conversion rates, and client acquisition expenses. By using data to inform decisions, this data-driven strategy guarantees that resources are directed toward the most productive channels and strategies for marketing campaigns.

Furthermore, a clearly defined marketing plan makes establishing a solid brand identity and positioning the company in the market easier. It enables companies to stand out from rivals by clearly and consistently articulating their distinctive value proposition across all platforms. A strong brand identity fosters customers' trust and loyalty, essential for long-term success in the e-commerce sector.

In summary, e-commerce marketing includes a variety of channels, each with extraordinary potential to increase traffic and revenue. Effectively utilizing various channels such as email marketing, social media, PPC, and SEO calls for a carefully thought-out marketing plan. With the help of this approach, all efforts are guaranteed to be coordinated, quantifiable, and impact-maximizing. E-commerce companies can improve their online presence, draw in more clients, and experience long-term success by implementing these marketing concepts.

SEO and Content Marketing

The cornerstones of digital marketing, search engine optimization (SEO) and content marketing, complement one another to increase a website's exposure and draw in natural traffic. To have a solid online presence and promote long-term growth, businesses must comprehend the fundamentals of SEO and the function of blogging and content creation in this regard.

SEO is optimizing a website to rank higher on search engine results pages (SERPs). Higher rankings make it more likely for users looking for pertinent content, goods, or services to find you organically—without paying for advertising. Making a website's content easily interpreted and indexed by search engines is the main objective of search engine optimization (SEO), which increases user accessibility. On-page, off-page, and technical SEO are three major categories into which effective SEO tactics and strategies fall.

Optimizing a single web page to improve its ranking and attract more relevant visitors is known as on-page SEO. The first of many essential components in this is keyword research. The first step is determining the keywords, words, and phrases that prospective clients will likely use while looking for similar goods or services. These keywords can be located with programs like Ahrefs, SEMrush, and Google Keyword Planner. Following their identification, these keywords should be thoughtfully inserted into the body text, meta descriptions, titles, and headings of the website's content to ensure they flow organically and don't interfere with the material's readability.

High-quality content is essential for on-page SEO. Content that is interesting, educational, and pertinent to users' search queries is given priority by search engines. This is where blogging and content creation—particularly content marketing—become essential. Publishing excellent blog entries, articles, and other content regularly can help a website become recognized as a reliable source in its industry. Every content piece offers the chance to focus on particular keywords, respond to frequently asked queries, and deliver value to the reader. Furthermore, quality content increases the likelihood of obtaining backlinks from other websites—an essential component of off-page SEO.

Activities that improve a website's authority and reputation outside its domain are called off-page SEO. Getting links from other reliable websites is known as backlink building, and it is the most essential component of off-page SEO. As endorsements, backlinks let search engines know that a piece of information is reliable and worthwhile. Creating shareable content that organically draws connections and guest blogging—writing content for other websites in exchange for a backlink—are two effective backlink techniques. Off-page SEO also benefits from social media involvement because widely shared and discussed material increases a website's authority and visibility.

Technical SEO concentrates on enhancing the backend functionality and structure of the website to increase its usability and visibility. Since many visitors access the internet via mobile devices, ensuring the website is mobile-friendly is one of the critical components of technical SEO. Websites optimized for mobile devices are ranked higher by search engines like Google. Site speed is vital; poorly designed websites can drive visitors away and hurt search engine rankings. To aid in search engine indexing, technical SEO also entails building a transparent, crawlable site architecture with a logical structure. Other crucial technical SEO procedures include putting safe HTTPS protocols into place and ensuring no broken links or duplicate material.

In content marketing, blogging is a potent instrument that aids SEO initiatives. Businesses can target a wide range of keywords and cover various topics relevant to their audience by regularly writing blog entries. Every blog post presents an opportunity to draw in multiple audience demographics and rank for new keywords. Additionally, blogging enables companies to interact with their community, establish credibility with their readers, and display their knowledge. Superior blog entries can be disseminated via social media networks, augmenting their scope and ability to draw in backlinks.

Blogging is just one aspect of content development; other mediums include podcasts, e-books, films, and infographics. Variety in content kinds accommodates varying audience tastes and consumption patterns. For example, infographics can improve understanding and simplify complex material, while films can be engaging and highly shareable. Podcasts are portable and provide a personal means of communication with listeners. Frequently employed as lead magnets, e-books, and whitepapers offer comprehensive insights on particular subjects and can facilitate the development of an email list of subscribers.

When creating content, consistency is essential. Frequent updates inform search engines that the website is live and always adding new content. A consistent flow of fresh content can be ensured by planning and coordinating content creation activities using an editorial calendar. Furthermore, content can be repurposed to increase its effect and reach. An example would be transforming a blog post into a video or infographic.

To sum up, search engine optimization and content marketing work hand in hand to create the framework for effective digital marketing campaigns. While content marketing, through blogging and creating varied content, fuels the engine by feeding the audience with valuable and captivating information, search engine optimization (SEO) lays the groundwork by optimizing a website's structure and content for search engines. Businesses may improve their online presence, draw in more organic visitors, and eventually accomplish their digital marketing goals by comprehending and putting into practice the fundamentals of SEO and including a strong content marketing plan.

Social Media Marketing

Social media marketing gives businesses an even greater chance to engage with their audience, increase brand recognition, and boost sales. It has become an essential part of digital marketing tactics. Social media marketing success depends on picking the appropriate channels to concentrate on and producing exciting content that appeals to the intended audience. Comprehending these facets is vital to optimizing social media usage.

The interests and behaviors of the target audience should be considered when choosing social media sites. Selecting platforms that align with the business's objectives and target audience is crucial because each has distinct features, user demographics, and content formats. For example, Facebook is one of the most popular platforms, with a large user base and powerful advertising possibilities. It works exceptionally well to reach a wide range of audiences and utilize precise targeting choices to target particular demographics. Facebook offers businesses many options to interact with their audience, advertise products, and foster a sense of community with its features, which include Pages, Groups, and Ads.

Another effective channel is Instagram, owned by Facebook, particularly for companies looking to market to younger consumers. Because of its visual-centric style, Instagram is great for brands that can use high-quality photos and videos to communicate their narrative. Instagram is a flexible platform for sharing behind-the-scenes content, presenting products, and enabling direct purchases, thanks to features like IGTV, Shopping, and

Stories. Instagram is the ideal medium for firms in the fashion, beauty, food, and lifestyle industries because of its focus on aesthetics and visual storytelling.

Because Twitter is real-time, it's great for businesses that want to communicate news, have quick conversations, and respond to customers. It works exceptionally well for companies looking to promote their websites, offer customer support, and get a voice in industry conversations. Twitter's brief layout promotes direct communication between brands and their audience and straightforward, powerful messaging.

For B2B marketing, LinkedIn is the preferred platform since it provides a polished setting for establishing connections with business executives, exchanging knowledgeable material, and developing a company brand. Businesses like technology, banking, and professional services can benefit most. LinkedIn offers organizations opportunities to build thought leadership, communicate with a professional audience, and generate leads through its features, which include Company Pages, LinkedIn Articles, and LinkedIn Ads.

Like Instagram, Pinterest is a visually focused site, but what sets it apart is its emphasis on inspiration and discovery. Businesses in categories where visual appeal and creativity drive engagement, like DIY, fashion, food, and home decor, might benefit significantly. Pinterest is a valuable tool for increasing traffic and sales because its users frequently utilize the platform for planning and making purchases.

The quickly expanding short-form video network TikTok presents a unique chance to connect with a younger, very interested audience. It is perfect for marketers producing engaging and viral content because its algorithm-driven content discovery feature can swiftly magnify content. Duets, challenges, and branded hashtags are just a few of the features on TikTok that can significantly increase user engagement and business exposure.

The next important step is to create exciting content when suitable platforms have been chosen. Effective social media marketing relies heavily on engaging content since it draws in viewers, promotes conversation, and helps them feel connected to the company. Understanding your audience's interests, tastes, and habits is essential to producing content that will engage them. Surveys, analytics, and direct audience interactions can all yield this knowledge.

Interactive media, such as surveys, assessments, and competitions, motivate viewers to participate actively. This kind of content engages users and offers insightful information about their ideas and preferences. To engage the audience and get feedback, a clothing manufacturer could, for instance, create a poll asking followers to vote on their favorite new design.

User-generated content (UGC) is an additional successful tactic. Authenticity and trust can be increased by allowing customers to repost and share their brand experiences. UGC serves as social proof, demonstrating to prospective buyers that other people have had good luck with the company. The brand's social media pages can use features, competitions, or hashtags to encourage this material.

Posting consistently is essential to preserving exposure and engagement. Planning and scheduling posts with an editorial calendar help guarantee a consistent material flow. Still, quality should be maintained for consistency. Every post need to offer something of worth, be it amusement, knowledge, or motivation.

Finally, using analytics to refine content strategies is essential. Social media platforms offer valuable information about the material's performance, the users interacting with it, and the content that appeals to them the most. These findings can guide future content creation to ensure it maximizes engagement and conforms to audience preferences.

A deliberate approach to platform selection and content generation is necessary for social media marketing. Companies can successfully engage their audience, foster brand loyalty, and spur expansion by concentrating on the appropriate channels and producing captivating, excellent content. To succeed in the continually changing social media world, one must be aware of the subtleties of each platform and constantly hone content strategy based on audience feedback and statistics.

Paid Advertising

An all-encompassing digital marketing plan must include paid advertising since it allows companies to efficiently and rapidly reach specific consumers. Google Ads, Facebook Ads, and influencer marketing are three of the most effective paid advertising strategies. Optimizing the efficacy of sponsored advertising campaigns requires a thorough understanding of these platforms and efficient budgeting and tracking of ROI.

One of the most well-known and influential online advertising systems is Google Ads, formerly Google AdWords. Using a pay-per-click (PPC) strategy, advertisers place bids on keywords related to their goods or services. Google places the adverts of the highest bidders at the top of the search results when consumers search for these keywords. Various campaign kinds are available with Google advertisements, such as search, display, video, retail, and app promotion advertisements. Search advertisements successfully capture users' intent to buy because they appear on Google's search engine results pages (SERPs). Conversely, display advertising reaches a wider audience by appearing on Google's extensive network of partner websites.

To optimize Google Ads' efficacy, careful keyword research is essential. Finding high-traffic keywords that are pertinent to the business might be aided by tools such as Google Keyword Planner. Advertisements should also be compelling and contain a clear call to action (CTA) to promote clicks. Additionally, Google Ads offers a wide range of targeting options, including device, demographic, and geographic targeting, which let advertisers more accurately reach the population they want to attract. To improve outcomes and return on investment, monitoring and optimizing ad performance through A/B testing continuously and modifying bids in response to keyword performance is essential.

A robust platform for connecting with a highly engaged audience is provided by Facebook Ads, a component of Meta's advertising ecosystem. Facebook ads target users based on their interests, activities, and demographics, unlike Google Ads, which target people based on their search queries. This enables the display of highly customized and aesthetically pleasing advertisements in user stories and news feeds, as well as throughout Facebook's network, which includes Instagram, Messenger, and Audience Network.

The success of an influencer marketing strategy depends on the choice of influencers. Influencers with audiences that fit their target demographic and whose ideals are consistent with their brand identity are the ones that brands should seek out. Compared to follower counts, engagement metrics—likes, comments, and shares—tell us how actively an influencer's audience engages with their material. Influencer campaigns come in various shapes and sizes, depending on the preferences of the influencer's audience and their style. Examples include sponsored posts, product reviews, unboxing, and giveaways.

To ensure that paid advertising campaigns are economical and provide quantifiable outcomes, efficient budgeting and ROI tracking are crucial. A comprehensive grasp of the expenses of various platforms and ad formats is essential to setting a budget for each campaign. Advertisers should consider cost-per-click (CPC) or cost-per-thousand-impressions (CPM) for Google Ads and Facebook Ads and base their budget allocation on anticipated CTR and conversion rates. The influencer's costs, which differ significantly depending on their reach and engagement levels, should be included in influencer marketing expenditures.

Measuring the return on investment from advertising expenditures is known as ROI tracking. Campaign performance may be understood by looking at key performance indicators (KPIs), including cost per acquisition (CPA), conversion rate, total return on ad spend (ROAS), and click-through rate (CTR). Robust analytics tools are provided by Google Ads and Facebook Ads, enabling advertisers to monitor these indicators and learn more about user behavior and the efficacy of their campaigns. Understanding how advertisements influence business outcomes is aided by conversion tracking, which entails setting up particular activities as targets, such as purchases or sign-ups.

Tracking ROI for influencer marketing can be more difficult, but it's still essential. Success can be gauged by metrics like engagement rates, traffic brought in by influencer posts, and sales due to influencer marketing. One helpful tool for immediately linking influencer efforts to sales is tracking links or special promo codes. Furthermore, conversions from influencer campaigns and referral traffic may be monitored using tools like Google Analytics.

In conclusion, influencer marketing, Facebook Ads, and Google Ads provide businesses with practical ways to connect with their target market and spur expansion. To maximize their impact, you must create interesting, targeted ads and grasp the subtleties of each platform. Strict ROI tracking offers performance insights and guides future strategy, while adequate budgeting guarantees that advertising expenditures align with campaign objectives. By integrating these components into a well-rounded digital marketing plan, companies can fully leverage paid advertising to accomplish their goals and foster long-term success.

CHAPTER VII

Converting Visitors to Customers

Understanding the Customer Journey

Any business must strive to turn visitors into customers, which is more critical in the digital age when customers have short attention spans and severe competition. Reaching this objective necessitates a thorough comprehension of the customer journey, which charts the steps a consumer takes from first awareness to last purchase. Businesses can develop a seamless and compelling experience that generates conversions and creates long-lasting customer relationships by understanding these stages and optimizing touchpoints and interactions.

The buyer's journey, often the customer's, consists of multiple stages. Usually, these phases consist of cognizance, deliberation, and selection. To effectively engage and convert the prospect, new methods and approaches are needed for each stage, representing a distinct phase in the customer's route to purchase.

Potential clients identify a need or issue at the first stage, awareness, and start looking for solutions. They might need to be acquainted with particular brands or goods. Instead, they are gathering data and investigating possibilities. Here, content marketing is essential because companies must offer insightful, helpful material that solves customers' problems and establishes their brand as an authority in the industry. Infographics, instructional videos, blog articles, and social media material are valuable resources for drawing viewers in and making the first move.

To ensure prospective clients can quickly locate pertinent material, optimizing the company's online presence for search engines (SEO) during the awareness stage is critical. Raise your website's search engine ranks and increase organic traffic by using focused keywords, producing excellent content, and constructing backlinks. In addition to increasing visibility, paid advertising—such as social media and Google Ads—can draw in users actively looking for content.

In the second phase, known as consideration, prospective clients assess various options and refine their selections. Now that they have more knowledge, they compare different goods and services to see which one best suits their needs. Companies should concentrate on giving thorough details and showcasing the distinctive value of their products. Prospects can make more informed judgments and get closer to purchasing using case studies, product comparisons, testimonials, and comprehensive guides.

Email marketing is beneficial when consumers are still considering their options. Through lead magnets or subscription forms, businesses may obtain email addresses and use them to nurture leads with relevant and tailored information. Automated email sequences that offer continuous value to the prospect and keep the brand at the forefront include welcome series, product suggestions, and instructional newsletters. Retargeting advertisements can remind prospective buyers of the goods they have previously seen, enticing them to return to the website and finish their transaction.

When the prospect reaches the last phase, the decision, it's time to make a buy. They have now reduced the options and seek confirmation that this is the best choice. Converting prospects into customers can be facilitated by attractive product descriptions, obvious and convincing calls to action (CTAs), and open pricing. Reducing perceived risk and encouraging quick action can also be accomplished by providing time-limited discounts, free trials, or money-back guarantees.

Optimizing the checkout process is critical during the decision-making phase. Cart abandonment rates can be considerably decreased with a smooth, frictionless user experience that includes several payment alternatives, clear instructions, and streamlined forms. Offering top-notch customer service via live chat, FAQs, and prompt assistance can also take care of any last-minute issues and help with the purchase choice.

Businesses must understand that a customer's journey only finishes with a purchase once they've passed these initial steps. Recurring business and fostering loyalty require post-purchase conversations and touchpoints. Loyalty programs, satisfaction surveys, and follow-up emails can all be used to keep people interested and build lasting relationships. Customers' testimonials and experience sharing on social media can be leveraged to increase brand advocacy and draw in new business.

Touchpoints and interactions are essential for directing prospects toward conversion at every stage of the customer experience. Any online or offline contacts a prospective customer has with the brand are called touchpoints. These can involve using social media, visiting websites, sending emails, responding to ads, and interacting with customer care. Every touchpoint offers a chance to sway customers' opinions and encourage them to purchase.

Businesses should use an omnichannel strategy to maximize touchpoints, guaranteeing a unified and consistent experience across all channels. This entails combining online and offline initiatives, such as coordinating in-store marketing with online campaigns or offering a smooth transition from a social media advertisement to a website. Additionally, personalization is essential because it can increase relevance and effect by customizing offers and messages depending on consumer behavior and preferences.

Mapping the customer journey is a valuable technique for locating and maximizing touchpoints. Through customer-centric journey mapping, businesses can identify possible pain points, gaps, and areas for improvement. To obtain insights into customers' behavior and preferences, this process entails evaluating data from various sources, including CRM systems, website analytics, and customer feedback. Regularly maintaining and improving the customer journey map guarantees that the company can adjust to changing market trends and client needs.

To sum up, turning visitors into customers necessitates a systematic approach that recognizes and attends to the many phases of the buyer's journey. By generating relevant information, touchpoint optimization, and personalized and engaging experiences, companies can successfully lead prospects from first awareness to ultimate purchase. Businesses may maintain alignment with customer needs and drive growth and conversions by routinely evaluating and improving the customer journey.

Optimizing Product Pages for Conversion

Conversion-optimized product pages are essential for e-commerce success. An effective product page can significantly influence a customer's choice to buy. Therefore, it's critical to concentrate on the vital components that encourage conversions. In this approach, effective call-to-actions (CTAs) and trust signals like testimonials and reviews are two of the most critical elements.

Call-to-actions are buttons or prompts that direct users to do particular actions, including clicking "Buy Now," "Add to Cart," or "Sign Up." These cues are vital in helping customers navigate the buying process. A clear, appealing, and well-placed call to action maximizes visibility and engagement. CTA language should be convincing and action-oriented. For example, a more compelling option like "Get Your Free Trial" can generate a sense of urgency and value instead of just using the generic "Submit" button. CTAs' color and style are also quite important. To make buttons stand out from the rest of the page, they should frequently be colored in contrasting hues that draw the eye. Furthermore, putting CTAs in strategic locations—like next to product descriptions and photos or inside the shopping cart—can improve user experience and boost conversion rates.

Credibility can be further increased by testimonials, particularly those provided by reliable sources or influential people. These can be included in product descriptions or displayed as stand-alone quotes. Video testimonials offer an additional level of authenticity by showcasing real people talking about their positive experiences in a way that potential consumers can see and hear. Furthermore, showing user-generated content can make the purchasing experience more relatable and exciting. This type of content includes images or videos of customers using the product.

Trust signals go beyond endorsements and ratings. Trust-building also heavily relies on promises, security badges, and certifications. Showing off security badges from reputable companies, such as SSL certifications or payment security emblems, gives consumers peace of mind that their financial and personal data is secure. Money-back guarantees or simple return procedures can ease worries about possible discontent, increasing the likelihood that buyers will finish their transaction.

Using trust signals from external review sites or prizes is another successful tactic. Displaying industry accolades, recognitions, and ratings from websites like Trustpilot or Google Reviews can help bolster a brand's legitimacy and quality of goods. Moreover, offering comprehensive product details, sharp photos, and videos can improve clarity and lower ambiguity. Consumers like complete product descriptions containing measurements, features, usage guidelines, and visual aids that provide a whole perspective of the item.

In conclusion, a strategic strategy centered on persuasive calls to action and trust signals is necessary for optimizing product pages for conversion. CTAs that are well-placed, appealing, and clear help clients through the purchasing process and motivate them to act immediately. Trust signals, such as endorsements, security badges, and reviews, inspire trust and reassure prospective customers about the dependability and quality of the products. Businesses may provide a more convincing and reliable purchasing experience on their product pages, increasing conversion rates and encouraging repeat business.

Cart Abandonment Strategies

A common problem in e-commerce is cart abandonment, where prospective buyers add products to their shopping carts but exit the website without purchasing. Conversion rates and income can be significantly increased by comprehending the reasons for cart abandonment and implementing appropriate recovery measures.

Several things lead to cart abandonment. Unexpected expenses are one of the leading causes. If extra costs, such as shipping, taxes, or other hidden costs, are discovered toward the end of the checkout process, customers could feel taken aback and choose not to finish the transaction. Companies should offer a clear and comprehensive cost breakdown early in the purchasing process, ideally on the product page or before the buyer gets to the checkout step, to lessen this.

A complicated or drawn-out checkout procedure is another frequent cause of cart abandonment. Consumers are frequently turned off by lengthy form fields, the need to create an account, or difficult to use navigation. Reducing abandonment rates can be achieved by streamlining the checkout process. The process can be simplified and more user-friendly by adding a guest checkout option, reducing the steps needed to complete a transaction, and using form fields with auto-fill features.

There are various strategies that firms can use to retrieve abandoned carts. Forwarding cart abandonment emails is one of the best strategies. Customers who leave products in their carts receive reminder emails, incentivizing them to return and finish their transactions. The first email should be sent as soon as possible after the abandonment; this is when timing matters most. These emails must be customized, emphasizing the particular products in the cart and offering a solid call to action.

Emails with incentives can increase the efficacy of cart abandonment campaigns. Customers can be enticed to complete their purchases by providing a discount, free shipping, or a particular campaign. Businesses should use incentives sparingly to prevent creating a precedent where customers come to expect a discount each time they leave a cart empty.

An additional effective strategy for reclaiming abandoned baskets is retargeting advertising. These advertisements remind consumers of their interest and entice them to return and finish their purchase by displaying the abandoned products. At the same time, they visit other websites or social media platforms. Retargeting advertisements can be highly customized according to the browsing and purchasing habits of the user, which raises the possibility of conversion.

Recovering abandoned carts can also benefit from live chat support. Consumers with queries or worries regarding the goods, shipping, or return procedures may leave their carts empty. By providing live chat support during the checkout process, you may lower the likelihood of cart abandonment by giving customers access to instant answers and reassurances. Chatbot technology can offer service around the clock, and typical questions can be answered quickly.

Given the rising percentage of consumers making purchases on smartphones and tablets, optimizing the checkout experience for mobile devices is imperative. Ensuring the website is responsive, has an easy-to-use layout, and is mobile-friendly will improve the purchasing experience and lower cart abandonment on mobile platforms.

Lastly, examining data on cart abandonment might offer insightful information about the precise moments when customers give up on their carts. Businesses may find and fix the root causes by tracking and analyzing these trends with analytics tools. A/B testing can be used to optimize the user experience and raise conversion rates for various checkout process components, such as form layouts, CTA buttons, and page designs.

In summary, cart abandonment is a complex problem that can be solved by combining knowledge of its root causes with practical recovery tactics. Businesses can lower cart abandonment rates by offering transparent pricing, streamlining the checkout procedure, guaranteeing website performance and security, and cultivating customer trust. Additionally, you may recover lost purchases and improve the overall buying experience by utilizing strategies like live chat assistance, retargeting ads, mobile optimization, and cart abandonment emails.

Enhancing Customer Experience

Improving the client experience is crucial for companies looking to create enduring bonds and encourage adherence. Exemplary customer service, which entails putting best practices that put responsiveness, empathy, and problem-solving first, is one of the critical components of accomplishing this. Businesses may create pleasant experiences that leave a lasting impression on customers by swiftly addressing and remedying customer concerns and issues.

Active listening and comprehension are the foundations of good customer service—consumers like being acknowledged and understood, particularly when facing difficulties or having particular requirements. Empathy is an essential part of the process for customer service workers to engage with consumers on a personal level and show sincere concern for their well-being. Businesses can establish rapport and trust with their consumers by understanding their circumstances and feelings, which paves the way for a satisfying customer experience.

Another crucial component of excellent customer service methods is timeliness. In contemporary times, clients anticipate rapid resolutions to their questions and concerns. Whether returning calls, sending emails, or attending to messages on social media, companies ought to offer prompt and effective service. By putting procedures and systems in place to handle and prioritize client requests, you can ensure that no customer has to wait around for a long time, increasing their happiness and decreasing their dissatisfaction.

Moreover, customization is essential for improving the client experience. Consumers value tailored communications considering their interests, past purchases, and special requirements. Businesses can customize their interactions and communications to personally connect with each consumer by utilizing customer data and insights. Customized messages, targeted offers, and personalized recommendations show that companies appreciate and know their clients, which builds a sense of connection and loyalty.

Improving the consumer experience also requires engagement. To cultivate relationships and promote loyalty, businesses should go above and beyond addressing problems and responding to queries. This can entail proactive outreach to get feedback and guarantee client happiness, including follow-up emails or surveys following a transaction. Social media platforms offer supplementary avenues for consumer engagement, enabling businesses to participate in real-time communication with customers, reply to messages and comments, and exhibit their brand values and personality.

Furthermore, it is imperative to maintain proactive communication to inform and engage clients at every stage of their journey. Proactive communication shows attention to detail and a dedication to customer satisfaction, whether it's updating consumers on the status of their orders, making appropriate product recommendations, or alerting them to impending discounts. Businesses may improve the overall experience and forge closer bonds with their clientele by keeping them informed and involved.

To sum up, improving the customer experience necessitates a multidimensional strategy that includes engagement, personalization, and best practices for customer service. Businesses can create memorable client experiences by emphasizing timeliness, empathy, and responsiveness in customer service interactions. By adjusting interactions and communications to each customer's tastes and needs, personalization enables firms to build a sense of connection and loyalty. Proactive interaction and communication also guarantee that clients feel appreciated and informed at every stage of the process, which improves the experience even more. By implementing these tactics, companies may stand out from the competition, cultivate enduring client relationships, and promote long-term success.

CHAPTER VIII
Scaling Your Drop Shipping Business

When to Scale

Growing your drop shipping company can be a game-changing move in the right direction for boosting sales and market share. Growing at the appropriate moment and properly is essential to ensure sustainable growth and stay clear of potential problems. This in-depth guide explores the vital markers that indicate whether your company is ready to grow and the steps you need to take to ensure a seamless and productive expansion process.

Rather than being motivated only by ambition, the decision to grow your drop shipping company should be based on particular signs. Consistent profitability is one of the critical indications. Your business concept may be successful and even thrive on a larger scale if it has been producing consistent earnings for a considerable time. Maintaining a consistent profit is more important than having occasional high-revenue periods since it shows how stable your business is and how much demand there is for your goods.

The capacity to effectively manage ongoing activities is another crucial factor. You may be prepared to scale if your business operations—from customer service to inventory management—function well and can handle higher volumes without sacrificing quality. A business can handle the higher demand without experiencing significant disruptions thanks to efficient operations when it expands.

Another crucial element is market demand. To make sure there is enough demand for your products, do extensive market research. Analyzing competition, market trends, and customer feedback is necessary for this. Scaling up could help you get a more significant market share if the market is expanding and there is a growing need for your items.

Before thinking about scaling, a robust supply chain is also necessary. It is essential to have dependable suppliers who can quickly process larger orders. A single weak point in the supply chain has the power to seriously disrupt operations, resulting in unhappy customers and maybe lost revenue. Make sure your suppliers can expand along with your company and are scalable.

Customer feedback is one of the most essential tools for determining whether to scale. Repeat business and positive reviews are good signs that your consumers are happy and have a devoted following willing to help you expand. You may focus on these areas as you grow by analyzing customer evaluations and conducting surveys to gain insights into what customers appreciate most about your products and services.

The saturation of your present market is another sign. It might be time to look into other markets if you've reached the peak of your market penetration and are having trouble bringing new clients to your current target market. If you target other client niches or expand regionally, there may be new growth prospects.

The factor of financial stability is non-negotiable. Scaling requires access to finance and a healthy cash flow. Investments in technology, marketing, and new hiring are all necessary for growth. Ensure you have a solid plan for handling rising costs without endangering the viability of your company's finances.

Enhancing your supply chain is an additional crucial measure. Build trusting relationships with suppliers and work out advantageous arrangements for higher order volumes. You can reduce the risk of supply disruptions by diversifying your source base. Ensure your shipping and logistics procedures are effective and can handle increasing volumes without experiencing delays.

It is essential to scale marketing and consumer acquisition efforts effectively. Set aside more money for digital marketing initiatives that involve email marketing, search engine optimization, and social media advertising. Using data analytics, you can more precisely target your advertising, make sure the correct people see them, and increase the return on your investment.

Managing expansion requires hiring the appropriate people. As your company grows, you'll need more workers to execute different tasks like operations, marketing, and customer support. Employing seasoned experts familiar with the complexities of raising a company can offer insightful advice and support in overcoming growth-related obstacles.

Lastly, it's critical to continue providing outstanding customer service while scaling. Growth should come at something other than the expense of the caliber of services you offer. To effectively handle the rising volume of client inquiries, implement scalable customer support solutions like chatbots and customer relationship management (CRM) systems. Ensuring customers have a good experience can help you draw in new business and keep your current clientele.

In conclusion, meticulous preparation and execution are necessary for growing your drop shipping company. You may guarantee that your expansion is effective and sustainable by identifying the appropriate signs and taking the necessary precautions. Key considerations include steady profitability, effective operations, sustainable market demand, and a robust supply chain. Your company can be ready for successful scaling if it makes the necessary preparations through strategic planning, technological investments, supply chain strengthening, efficient marketing, and employing the right staff.

Strategies for Scaling

A strategic approach is needed for a business to scale and experience sustained growth and increased profitability. Adding new products to the lineup and breaking into untapped areas are the two main approaches to development. Both tactics provide particular chances and difficulties, and when used well, they can significantly increase the clientele and income of your company.

Adding additional items to your current line is expanding your product line. This tactic can draw in more clients, boost revenue from current clients, and lessen the danger of depending unduly on a small range of goods. An essential component of any successful product range expansion is comprehensive market research. Gaining insight into consumer behavior, market trends, and product gaps can enable you to find possible goods that will appeal to your target market. Making educated judgments can also be facilitated by examining competitors' product offerings since this can offer valuable insights into what works and what doesn't.

The next stage is to validate these concepts after discovering possible products. This can be accomplished through surveys, focus groups, or pre-orders to determine consumer interest. Before making a complete commitment, product ideas should be validated to save costs and guarantee that there is a market for the new offerings. In addition, before increasing production, consider launching a limited edition or small batch to gauge consumer reaction.

When growing your product line, marketing must be done well. Utilize your current consumer base by using social media, email marketing, and other methods to tell them about the new offerings. To entice customers to make their first purchase, emphasize the new products' specific qualities and advantages and consider providing exclusive deals or discounts. Collaborating with influencers and using influencer marketing can also help spread the word and reach more people.

Conducting thorough market research is crucial before venturing into a novel industry. This entails being aware of the market's size, potential for growth, client demographics, subtle cultural differences, and competitive environment. It would be easier to adjust your products and marketing techniques if you could determine the particular requirements and preferences of the clients in the new market.

Numerous logistical factors are involved in geographic growth. Evaluating the new market's regulatory landscape is one of the initial stages. This entails being aware of tax laws, import/export policies, and other legal obligations. Forming local alliances or collaborating with regional distributors might assist in navigating these challenges and offer insightful information about the industry.

Localization is essential when expanding into new markets. This extends beyond simply localizing your website and promotional materials. It entails customizing your offerings, costs, and customer support to the unique requirements and inclinations of the regional market. Your cultural sensitivity and awareness can significantly impact your ability to succeed in a new market.

Reaching new markets requires the use of digital marketing. Reaching potential clients and increasing brand recognition can be achieved by utilizing influencers, search engines, and local social media platforms. Your marketing campaigns will be more effective if you design them to appeal to the local audience. Furthermore, contemplate utilizing regional gatherings, conventions, and collaborations to enhance awareness and legitimacy within the novel industry.

A strong logistics network is also necessary for market expansion. To satisfy customers and guarantee on-time delivery, shipping, warehousing, and fulfillment procedures must be carried out effectively. Using regional logistics, companies can save expenses and increase productivity.

Another important consideration when entering new markets is customer service. Client happiness and loyalty can be enhanced by offering localized customer service, which includes language options and an understanding of local customs. Purchasing customer relationship management (CRM) software can assist in managing client communications and offering tailored experiences.

When entering new markets, risk management and financial preparation are essential. This entails establishing precise financial objectives, allocating funds for advertising and operational costs, and controlling currency exchange risks. You can reduce the dangers connected with variations in demand or the state of the economy in a particular market by diversifying your sources of income.

In conclusion, a lot of growth potential may be unlocked by scaling your firm through product range expansion and market entry. Careful preparation, in-depth market research, and effective execution are necessary for both tactics. Understanding market trends, vetting product concepts, effective marketing, and running your business profitably are all essential to diversifying your product offering. Thorough market research, localization, digital marketing, reliable logistics, and top-notch customer support are required when venturing into new markets. You may achieve long-term success and sustainable growth for your organization by implementing these methods and keeping an eye on your customers' needs and market dynamics.

Outsourcing and Delegation

Delegation and outsourcing are essential tactics for successfully growing a firm. Owners of businesses can concentrate on their core competencies and strategic expansion by assigning specific work to agencies or freelancers. This handbook examines the kinds of jobs that can be outsourced and offers advice on locating and overseeing independent contractors or agencies to guarantee fruitful collaborations.

The first step to effective delegation is determining which jobs are appropriate to outsource. Time-consuming, routine jobs that don't directly support your company's core skills are excellent candidates for outsourcing. Administrative duties, including data entry, scheduling, and customer service, are a few examples. Business owners can free up time to concentrate on strategic decision-making and business development by outsourcing these tasks.

Another area where outsourcing can be beneficial is in marketing chores. Specialized knowledge of current trends and algorithms is necessary for SEO, social media management, content production, digital marketing, and other fields. Hiring professionals to handle these responsibilities may increase the impact of marketing initiatives and maintain your company's competitiveness. It is also possible to outsource graphic design and video production, frequently required for marketing materials, to experts in the creative industries.

While they might not call for full-time internal employees, technical duties like website development, maintenance, and IT assistance are essential to the efficient running of your company. By contracting with independent contractors or specialized organizations, you can avoid the overhead expenses of hiring full-time staff and maintain a modern and robust IT infrastructure. Furthermore, technological jobs like software development, app creation, and cybersecurity can be outsourced to experts with the required abilities, as they frequently call for high competence.

Bookkeeping, payroll processing, tax preparation, and other routine financial chores are essential but can be outsourced. Qualified accountants and financial services firms can effectively handle these responsibilities, guaranteeing accuracy and regulatory compliance. This lowers the possibility of mistakes and possible legal problems in addition to saving time.

Finding the ideal freelancers or agencies comes next after you have decided which duties to outsource. A worldwide pool of independent contractors with various skill sets is accessible through websites such as Upwork, Freelancer, and Fiverr. These platforms simplify identifying skilled experts who meet your demands by letting you browse portfolios, read client testimonials, and compare prices.

You can also identify trustworthy freelancers or agencies by attending business events, networking in industry-specific forums, and asking colleagues for references. Personal recommendations frequently include a guarantee of previous excellent performance, which makes it simpler to entrust important work to the outsourced partner.

Researching an agency thoroughly is crucial when thinking about one. Examine their case studies and portfolios to learn about their experience and qualifications. Reviews and testimonials from clients might reveal information about their dependability and caliber of work. To further understand previous clients' experiences and satisfaction levels, think about contacting references and having direct conversations with them.

Reviews of performance and feedback are crucial for preserving quality and enhancing subsequent partnerships. When giving constructive criticism for a task that has been accomplished, make sure to point out both the good and the bad. Frequent performance assessments can assist agencies or independent contractors in comprehending your expectations and making steady progress toward them.

Developing a long-term partnership with dependable agencies or freelancers can offer continuity and a better comprehension of your company's objectives. When you locate experts who produce high-quality work, you should set up retainer or continuous contracts. This guarantees that you have dependable assistance when required and cultivates fidelity and a more robust dedication to your enterprise.

It's crucial to be explicit about payment and contract conditions. Ensure that all critical parts of the working relationship, such as deliverables, project dates, and payment terms, are outlined in a formal agreement. In addition to offering both parties legal protection, this helps to prevent misunderstandings.

Finally, delegating and outsourcing are effective business growth and efficiency techniques. Business owners can concentrate on their core competencies and strategic expansion by determining which jobs are appropriate for outsourcing and locating qualified freelancers or agencies. Successful outsourcing requires good management, transparent communication, and the development of enduring relationships. By implementing these tactics, companies can improve operations and promote long-term success by utilizing outside knowledge.

Advanced Marketing Techniques

In the cutthroat world of digital marketing, sophisticated strategies like affiliate marketing, email marketing, and retargeting have become indispensable resources for companies trying to increase their reach and conversion rates. Every tactic has a unique collection of tactics and best practices that, when combined, can form a practical marketing toolkit.

A compelling tactic for re-engaging potential customers who have already connected with your brand but did not finish a desired action—like completing a purchase or signing up for a service—is retargeting. This method shows targeted advertisements to these users while they explore other websites or social media networks. Retargeting's main objective is to keep your brand in front of consumers' minds and entice them to revisit your website and become customers.

The secret to retargeting's success is its capacity to exploit user data to produce tailored ad experiences. Through cookies, marketers can monitor how users behave on a website and categorize them according to their actions. For instance, advertisements showing a particular product, possibly with a unique price or offer, may be sent to a user who viewed it but did not buy it. Because the adverts are highly relevant to the user's interests, this level of customization significantly boosts conversion possibilities.

With dynamic retargeting, personalization is increased by automatically creating advertisements featuring goods or services the customer has already looked at. This method works exceptionally well for e-commerce companies with a lot of inventory since it makes creating personalized adverts on a wide scale possible. Dynamic retargeting helps shorten the sales cycle and recoup potentially lost purchases by persistently reminding potential customers of their initial interest.

Email marketing is still one of the most efficient and successful digital marketing techniques; through individualized and targeted messaging, businesses interact directly with their audience, building relationships and encouraging conversions. Building a high-quality email list, properly segmenting that list, and providing insightful content that appeals to each segment are the keys to successful email marketing.

Providing prospective subscribers with value is the first step in developing your email list. This could take the shape of access to special events, discounts, or unique material. You should carefully consider where to put opt-in forms on your blog, website, and social media pages to draw readers in and entice them to subscribe.

Once your email list is extensive and active, segmentation becomes essential. Depending on demographics, behavior, and preferences, you may segment your list into smaller, more focused groups and customize your communications to each group's unique needs and interests. For example, a welcome series introducing your company to new subscribers might be sent, while loyalty awards or customized product recommendations could be sent to returning consumers.

An essential component of successful email marketing is personalization. It entails sending content pertinent to the recipient's interests and habits and using their name. Sophisticated email marketing platforms facilitate mass customization and automation, allowing companies to send highly targeted messages based on user behavior, including browsing history, prior purchases, and email interaction.

For ongoing development, tracking the effectiveness of your email marketing initiatives is crucial. Important indicators like open, click-through, conversion, and unsubscribe rates offer insightful information about what is and is not working. You can improve the effectiveness of your campaigns overall, hone your tactics, and enhance your content by examining these indicators.

Sustaining robust connections with your affiliates is crucial for sustained prosperity. Maintaining open communication lines, making timely payments, and praising their work will foster loyalty and motivate them to keep promoting your business. Continuing assistance and resources can also help affiliates increase sales and perform better.

To sum up, cutting-edge marketing strategies like affiliate marketing, email marketing, and retargeting effectively boost your advertising campaigns and reach your objectives. Email marketing encourages direct, tailored contact, retargeting aids in re-engaging potential clients, and affiliate programs broaden your reach through collaborations depending on performance. Businesses may develop a comprehensive and coherent marketing strategy that promotes engagement, conversions, and long-term growth by successfully implementing these techniques.

CHAPTER IX

Managing Finances and Legal Aspects

Setting Up Business Finances

Managing finances and legal aspects is critical for the success and sustainability of any business. Proper financial management and adherence to legal requirements help companies maintain a clear picture of their financial health, meet regulatory obligations, and avoid legal pitfalls. This comprehensive guide explores setting up business finances, opening accounts, and understanding basic accounting principles.

Setting up business finances involves establishing a robust financial framework that supports your business's smooth operation and growth. The first step in this process is creating a business plan that includes financial projections. These projections should outline expected revenue, expenses, and profitability over the first few years. A well-thought-out financial plan helps you anticipate cash flow needs and secure funding from investors or lenders.

Once you have a financial plan, it's essential to establish a budgeting process. A budget acts as a financial roadmap, guiding your spending and allocating resources efficiently. Regularly updating and reviewing your budget allows you to track performance against your projections and make necessary adjustments.

Incorporating your business as a legal entity, such as a corporation or limited liability company (LLC), can provide financial and legal benefits. Incorporation separates your finances from your business finances, offering protection against personal liability for business debts and legal actions. It also enhances your credibility with customers, suppliers, and potential investors.

Opening business accounts is a fundamental step in managing your business finances effectively. A dedicated business bank account helps you separate personal and business transactions, simplifying bookkeeping and ensuring accurate financial records. When choosing a bank for your business account, consider fees, transaction limits, and the availability of business-specific services like merchant accounts and credit lines.

A business checking account is essential for daily operations, allowing you to deposit revenue, pay bills, and manage payroll. Some companies also benefit from a savings account, which can help manage cash reserves and earn interest on surplus funds. A business credit card can also help manage short-term expenses, track purchases, and build a business credit history.

Establishing a merchant account is crucial if your business accepts credit and debit card payments. A merchant account enables you to process card transactions securely, providing convenience to your customers and improving cash flow. Many banks offer integrated merchant services, simplifying the process of managing sales and transactions.

Understanding basic accounting principles is essential for maintaining accurate financial records and making informed business decisions. Accounting principles provide a framework for recording, reporting, and analyzing financial transactions, ensuring consistency and transparency in your financial statements.

Managing finances and legal aspects is a cornerstone of business success. Setting up business finances with a clear plan, budget, and incorporation helps create a solid financial foundation. Opening dedicated business accounts ensures the separation of personal and business finances, facilitating accurate bookkeeping and financial management. Understanding and applying basic accounting principles provides the framework for consistent, transparent, and accurate financial reporting. By adhering to these practices, businesses can maintain financial health, comply with regulatory requirements, and make informed decisions that drive growth and sustainability.

Budgeting and Financial Planning

Effective budgeting and financial planning are crucial for the success and sustainability of any business. These processes provide a roadmap for managing resources, setting financial goals, and making informed decisions. This comprehensive guide explores the intricacies of creating a budget and forecasting sales and expenses, key components that together form the backbone of sound financial management.

Creating a budget involves developing a detailed plan that outlines how your business will allocate its resources over a specific period, usually a year. The budgeting process starts with setting clear financial goals that align with your overall business objectives. These goals include increasing revenue, reducing costs, or saving for future investments. By defining these goals upfront, you can ensure that your budget supports your strategic priorities.

The next step in creating a budget is to gather historical financial data. Analyzing past performance provides a baseline for forecasting future revenues and expenses. This data includes income statements, balance sheets, and cash flow statements from previous years. Understanding historical trends helps identify patterns, seasonal fluctuations, and areas for improvement.

Revenue projections are a critical component of the budgeting process. Start by estimating your sales for the upcoming period. This involves considering factors such as market conditions, economic trends, competitive landscape, and marketing strategies. For established businesses, historical sales data can be a reliable indicator of future performance. For new businesses, market research and industry benchmarks can provide valuable insights.

Once you have projected your revenues, the next step is to estimate your expenses. Categorize expenses into fixed and variable costs. Fixed costs, such as rent, salaries, and insurance, remain relatively constant regardless of sales volume. Variable costs, such as raw materials, production costs, and sales commissions, fluctuate with changes in sales.

Market analysis is also crucial for sales forecasting. Assess the current market conditions, including economic indicators, industry trends, and competitive dynamics. Understanding these factors helps gauge potential demand for your products or services. For instance, if the economy is expected to grow, consumer spending may increase, boosting your sales prospects. Conversely, economic downturns may lead to decreased demand, necessitating more conservative sales projections.

Customer insights are another valuable input for sales forecasting. Gather feedback from your existing customers to understand their future purchasing intentions. Customer surveys, focus groups, and sales team insights can provide qualitative data that complements quantitative analysis. Additionally, monitor your sales pipeline and track the progress of leads and opportunities. This helps estimate the likelihood of closing deals and achieving your sales targets.

Expense forecasting involves predicting future costs based on historical data and anticipated changes. Start by analyzing your historical expense data to identify patterns and trends. Break down expenses into categories, such as cost of goods sold (COGS), operating expenses, and non-operating expenses. This detailed analysis helps pinpoint cost drivers and areas where efficiencies can be gained.

Identify areas where costs can be reduced or controlled without compromising quality or performance. This might involve negotiating better terms with suppliers, optimizing production processes, or implementing energy-saving initiatives. Regularly reviewing and adjusting your expense forecasts helps ensure they remain accurate and relevant.

Budgeting and financial planning are essential practices for managing a business's economic health and achieving long-term success. Creating a budget involves setting financial goals, projecting revenues and expenses, and developing a budgeted income statement. Accurate sales and expense forecasting, supported by historical data, market analysis, and customer insights, provides a solid foundation for your budget. By continuously monitoring and adjusting your forecasts, you can navigate financial challenges, seize opportunities, and steer your business toward sustainable growth.

Legal Considerations

Navigating the legal landscape is critical to establishing and running a successful business. Among the essential legal considerations are obtaining the necessary business licenses and permits and understanding the complexities of taxes and duties. These components ensure that your business operates legally and avoids potential fines, penalties, or disruptions.

The appropriate business licenses and permits are fundamental to setting up a business. Federal, state, and local governments require these licenses and permits to ensure companies comply with regulations, zoning laws, and industry-specific standards. The type of licenses and permits needed varies widely depending on the nature of your business, its location, and the industry in which it operates.

At the federal level, businesses in specific regulated industries, such as agriculture, alcohol, firearms, and aviation, may require particular licenses or permits. For example, companies manufacturing, importing, or selling guns and ammunition must obtain a Federal Firearms License from the Bureau of Alcohol, Tobacco, Firearms and Explosives (ATF). Similarly, businesses involved in producing or selling alcoholic beverages need to comply with regulations from the Alcohol and Tobacco Tax and Trade Bureau (TTB).

State business license and permit requirements can also be extensive and vary significantly. Most states require businesses to register with the state's revenue department or tax authority to collect sales tax. Professional licenses may be necessary for specific occupations, such as healthcare providers, lawyers, and accountants. Additionally, states may require environmental permits for businesses that engage in activities that could impact the environment, such as manufacturing or waste disposal.

Local governments, including cities and counties, typically have licensing and permitting requirements. Joint local permits include zoning permits, which ensure that a business's location complies with local zoning laws, and health permits for companies in the food and beverage industry. Home-based businesses may also need special permits or approvals from local authorities.

The process of obtaining business licenses and permits involves identifying the specific requirements for your business, completing the necessary applications, and paying applicable fees. It's crucial to research thoroughly and consult with legal experts or local government offices to ensure compliance with all relevant regulations. Please obtain the necessary licenses and permits to avoid fines, legal action, and potentially the closure of your business.

Understanding and managing taxes and duties is another critical legal consideration for businesses. Taxes are levied by federal, state, and local governments and can include income tax, sales tax, payroll tax, and property tax. Duties are tariffs or taxes imposed on imported and exported goods regulated by customs authorities.

Federal income tax is one of the primary taxes that businesses must manage. The Internal Revenue Service (IRS) requires companies to file annual tax returns and pay taxes on their income. The type of tax return a business files depends on its legal structure. For example, sole proprietorships file Schedule C with their tax return, while corporations file Form 1120. Partnerships and multi-member LLCs file Form 1065, with individual partners reporting their share of income on their tax returns.

State income tax varies by state, with some states imposing their corporate income tax while others do not tax business income at all. Additionally, most states impose sales tax on goods and services. Businesses must collect sales tax from customers at the point of sale and remit it to the state revenue department. The specific rate and rules for sales tax collection depend on the state and sometimes the locality.

Payroll taxes are another significant tax obligation for businesses with employees. These taxes include federal and state income tax withholding, Social Security and Medicare taxes (collectively known as FICA), and federal and state unemployment taxes. Employers are responsible for withholding the appropriate amounts from employees' wages, remitting these taxes to the relevant authorities, and filing periodic payroll tax returns.

Local governments levy property taxes on real estate and, in some cases, business personal property such as machinery and equipment. The amount of property tax owed is based on the assessed value of the property and the local tax rate. Businesses must ensure they accurately report their property holdings and pay the required taxes to avoid penalties.

Customs authorities regulate duties on imported and exported goods and can significantly impact businesses engaged in international trade. Import duties are taxes imposed on goods brought into a country, calculated based on the goods' value, type, and origin. Although less common, export duties are taxes on goods shipped out of a country. Businesses must comply with customs regulations, accurately classify their goods, and pay the appropriate duties to avoid fines and delays.

Businesses should implement robust accounting and record-keeping systems to manage taxes and duties effectively. Accurate financial records are essential for preparing tax returns, calculating tax liabilities, and providing documentation in the event of an audit. Consulting with tax professionals and legal experts can also help ensure compliance with tax laws and optimize tax planning strategies.

In conclusion, managing the legal considerations of business licenses, permits, taxes, and duties is essential for a business's lawful and efficient operation. Obtaining the necessary licenses and permits requires thorough research and compliance with federal, state, and local regulations. Understanding and managing taxes and duties involves staying informed about tax obligations at all levels of government and maintaining accurate financial records. By addressing these legal aspects diligently, businesses can avoid legal issues, enhance their credibility, and focus on growth and success.

Protecting Your Business

Protecting your business is a multifaceted endeavor that involves safeguarding intellectual property (IP) and effectively managing disputes and fraud. Intellectual property rights provide legal protection for creations of the mind. At the same time, a proactive approach to disputes and fraud can mitigate risks and preserve the integrity and reputation of your business. This comprehensive guide explores strategies for protecting intellectual property and handling disputes and fraud.

Intellectual property refers to creations such as inventions, designs, logos, names, and artistic works with commercial value. Protecting IP is essential for maintaining competitive advantage and ensuring others do not exploit your innovations and brand identity.

Protect new inventions and provide the patent holder with the exclusive right to manufacture, use, and sell the invention for a specified period, typically 20 years. The invention must be novel, non-obvious, and applicable to obtain a patent. The patent application process involves detailed documentation and examination by the patent office to determine eligibility. Once granted, a patent prevents others from making, using, or selling the invention without permission, allowing the inventor to capitalize on their innovation.

Protect symbols, names, logos, and slogans that distinguish goods or services. Registering a trademark provides legal protection and exclusive rights to use the mark in connection with the goods or services it represents. This protection helps prevent competitors from using similar marks that could confuse consumers. The trademark registration process involves a thorough search to ensure the mark is not already used and an application to the relevant authorities, such as the United States Patent and Trademark Office (USPTO).

Protect original works of authorship, such as literature, music, art, and software, from unauthorized copying, distribution, and performance. Copyright protection is automatic upon the creation of the work. However, registering the copyright with the appropriate office, such as the U.S. Copyright Office, provides additional legal benefits, including the ability to sue for damages in case of infringement.

Encompass confidential business information that provides a competitive edge, such as formulas, processes, and customer lists. Protecting trade secrets involves implementing robust security measures, including non-disclosure agreements (NDAs) with employees and partners, restricted access to sensitive information, and internal policies to prevent leaks.

Business disputes can arise from various sources, including contractual disagreements, employee issues, and competitor conflicts. Effective dispute-resolution strategies are crucial for minimizing disruptions and maintaining business relationships.

Fraud poses a significant threat to businesses, with the potential to cause financial loss, damage reputation, and erode customer trust. Implementing proactive measures to prevent, detect, and respond to fraud is crucial for protecting your business.

A swift and thorough response is essential when fraud is suspected or detected. Conducting an internal investigation to gather evidence and determine the extent of the scam is the first step. Engaging forensic accountants and legal experts can provide valuable assistance in this process. Reporting the scam to law enforcement and regulatory authorities may be necessary if the fraud involves significant financial loss or criminal activity.

In conclusion, protecting your business requires a comprehensive approach that includes safeguarding intellectual property, effectively managing disputes, and implementing robust fraud prevention measures. Intellectual property rights protect your innovations and brand identity, while proactive dispute resolution strategies and solid internal controls help maintain business integrity. By staying vigilant and prepared, businesses can navigate legal challenges and protect their assets, reputation, and long-term success.

CHAPTER X

Case Studies and Success Stories

Learning from Successful Drop Shippers

Understanding the strategies and tactics employed by successful drop shippers can provide valuable insights and practical lessons for those looking to thrive in the competitive world of e-commerce. Detailed case studies of accomplished drop shipping businesses highlight key takeaways and lessons that can be applied to achieve similar success.

Gymshark, a fitness apparel brand, is one of the most prominent success stories in the drop shipping industry. Established in 2012 by Ben Francis, Gymshark began as a drop shipping business, focusing on selling fitness supplements and later transitioning to gym apparel.

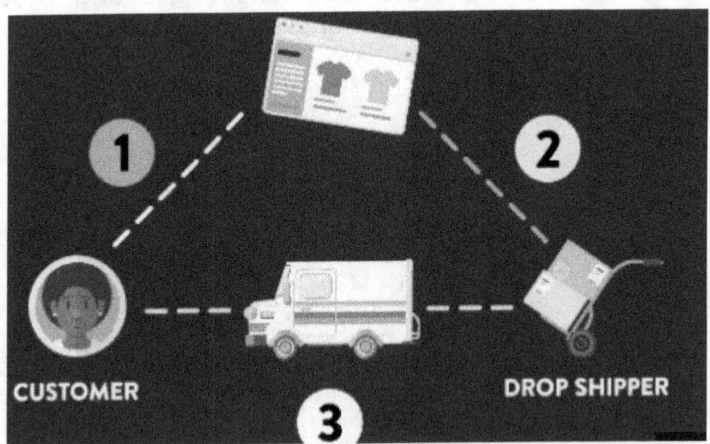

Gymshark's success can be attributed to several key factors. First, the brand leveraged social media, particularly Instagram and YouTube, to build a strong community around fitness enthusiasts. By partnering with fitness influencers and creating high-quality content, Gymshark was able to reach a large audience quickly and build a loyal customer base. This influencer marketing strategy drove traffic to their online store and enhanced brand credibility.

Another significant factor was Gymshark's focus on product quality and innovation. By closely listening to their community's feedback, they continuously improved their product line, ensuring that their offerings met their customers' specific needs and preferences. This customer-centric approach helped Gymshark differentiate itself in a crowded market.

Building a solid online presence through social media and influencer partnerships can significantly increase brand visibility and credibility. Continuously improving products based on customer feedback ensures high satisfaction and loyalty.

Oberlo, a drop shipping app for Shopify, showcases the power of providing solutions to common challenges drop shippers face. Founded by Tomas Slimas, Oberlo simplifies the process of finding products and suppliers, automating much of the drop shipping workflow.

Oberlo's success lies in its ability to streamline the drop shipping process for entrepreneurs. By offering a platform that integrates seamlessly with Shopify, Oberlo enables users to easily import products from suppliers, manage orders, and handle inventory without extensive technical knowledge. This convenience has made it a go-to solution for many drop shippers looking to scale their operations efficiently.

Oberlo also invests heavily in education and support, providing extensive resources such as tutorials, webinars, and customer support to help users succeed. This commitment to customer success has built a loyal user base and contributed to Oberlo's rapid growth.

A user-friendly platform addressing common pain points can attract and retain customers. Helping customers succeed through educational resources and support can build loyalty and drive growth.

Blenders Eyewear, founded by Chase Fisher, is another example of a successful drop shipping business that transitioned into a global brand. Initially starting with a small investment and focusing on selling stylish, affordable sunglasses, Blenders Eyewear leveraged social media and digital marketing to grow its customer base.

One of the critical strategies that led to Blenders Eyewear's success was its focus on branding and storytelling. By creating a brand narrative that resonated with a young, active lifestyle audience, Blenders Eyewear was able to differentiate itself from competitors. Their vibrant, high-energy marketing campaigns and consistent brand image helped them build a solid emotional connection with their customers.

Additionally, Blenders Eyewear employed data-driven marketing strategies. They continuously optimized their marketing campaigns and product offerings by analyzing customer data and feedback to meet customer preferences better. This data-driven approach allowed them to allocate marketing resources and achieve higher conversion rates efficiently.

MVMT Watches, founded by Jake Kassan and Kramer LaPlante, is a notable drop shipping success story that became a multi-million dollar brand. The company started by identifying a gap in the market for affordable, stylish watches and used drop shipping to test their product idea without significant upfront investment.

MVMT's growth strategy heavily relied on direct-to-consumer (DTC) marketing. MVMT could offer high-quality products at competitive prices by cutting out intermediaries and selling directly to consumers. Their marketing efforts focused on social media platforms, particularly Instagram, where they showcased their products with high-quality visuals and targeted ads.

Another factor contributing to MVMT's success was their use of crowdfunding platforms like Indiegogo to raise initial capital and validate their product concept. This approach gave them the funds needed to scale and build a community of early supporters who became brand advocates.

Selling directly to consumers can reduce costs and increase profit margins. Crowdfunding can be an effective way to raise funds and validate product concepts before scaling.

These case studies of Gymshark, Oberlo, Blenders Eyewear, and MVMT Watches offer valuable lessons for aspiring drop shippers. Key strategies include leveraging social media and influencers, focusing on product quality and innovation, simplifying the user experience, investing in customer education, creating strong brand narratives, using data-driven marketing, embracing direct-to-consumer models, and utilizing crowdfunding for validation and capital. By learning from these successful drop shippers, businesses can adopt proven tactics and strategies to enhance their chances of success in the competitive e-commerce landscape.

Common Pitfalls and How to Avoid Them

Navigating the landscape of entrepreneurship is fraught with challenges, and understanding common pitfalls can be instrumental in avoiding costly mistakes. By learning from the experiences of others and implementing strategies to overcome these challenges, entrepreneurs can increase their chances of success. This comprehensive guide explores some of the most common pitfalls faced by business owners and provides strategies to avoid them.

One of the most common pitfalls for entrepreneurs is failing to conduct thorough market research before launching their business. Without a clear understanding of their target market, competitors, and industry trends, entrepreneurs risk investing time and resources into products or services that may not meet market demand.

Financial mismanagement is another common pitfall that can derail businesses of all sizes. Whether it's underestimating startup costs, overspending on unnecessary expenses, or failing to maintain accurate financial records, poor financial management can lead to cash flow problems, debt accumulation, and ultimately, business failure.

Many businesses struggle due to ineffective marketing strategies. Whether it's a lack of targeting, inconsistent messaging, or insufficient promotion, failing to reach and engage the target audience can hinder growth and profitability.

In today's rapidly evolving business landscape, adaptability is key to survival. Businesses that fail to adapt to changing market conditions, consumer preferences, and technological advancements risk becoming obsolete.

The success of a business often hinges on the leadership and management capabilities of its founders and executives. Poor leadership can manifest in various ways, including indecision, micromanagement, lack of communication, and failure to delegate effectively.

Before launching a business or introducing a new product or service, invest time and resources into conducting comprehensive market research. Identify your target market, understand their needs and preferences, and assess the competitive landscape. Use data-driven insights to inform your business strategy and mitigate risks associated with market uncertainty.

Establish robust financial management practices from the outset of your business. Develop a realistic budget, track expenses diligently, and monitor cash flow regularly. Consider working with a financial advisor or accountant to ensure compliance with tax regulations, optimize financial performance, and mitigate risks associated with poor financial management.

Invest in developing a strategic marketing plan that aligns with your business goals and objectives. Define your target audience, identify key messages and channels, and develop compelling marketing campaigns that resonate with your target market.

Embrace a culture of adaptability and innovation within your organization. Stay informed about industry trends, emerging technologies, and changing consumer preferences. Encourage experimentation and creativity among your team members and be willing to pivot and adapt your business strategy in response to new opportunities and challenges.

Invest in developing strong leadership and management capabilities within your organization. Provide leadership training and mentorship opportunities for key personnel, foster open communication and collaboration, and lead by example. Cultivate a positive work culture that values accountability, integrity, and continuous improvement. By implementing strategies to mitigate these risks and challenges, businesses can position themselves for long-term growth and sustainability.

Future Trends in Drop Shipping

Anticipating future trends in drop shipping and e-commerce is essential for businesses to stay ahead of the curve and remain competitive in a rapidly evolving landscape. Emerging technologies, changing consumer behaviors, and market dynamics are reshaping the industry, presenting both challenges and opportunities for entrepreneurs.

Artificial intelligence and machine learning are revolutionizing the e-commerce industry by enabling personalized shopping experiences, predictive analytics, and automated customer service. AI-powered chatbots and virtual assistants can engage with customers in real-time, providing personalized recommendations and assistance throughout the shopping journey.

Augmented reality and virtual reality technologies are transforming the way consumers interact with products online. By overlaying digital content onto the physical world, AR enables customers to visualize products in their own environment before making a purchase, enhancing the online shopping experience and reducing returns. VR, on the other hand, immerses users in virtual environments, allowing them to explore products and environments in a more interactive and engaging way.

Voice commerce, enabled by virtual assistants like Amazon Alexa and Google Assistant, is gaining traction as consumers increasingly use voice-enabled devices to shop online. Voice commerce simplifies the purchasing process by allowing users to place orders and make transactions using voice commands, without the need for screens or keyboards.

Consumers are becoming increasingly conscious of environmental and social issues, driving demand for sustainable and ethically sourced products. Drop shippers that prioritize sustainability and ethical practices in their supply chain, packaging, and operations stand to gain a competitive advantage and appeal to environmentally and socially conscious consumers.

Omnichannel retailing, which involves seamlessly integrating multiple channels such as online, mobile, social media, and physical stores, is becoming the norm in e-commerce. Consumers expect a consistent and cohesive shopping experience across all channels, from browsing products online to making purchases in-store or via mobile apps.

Stay abreast of emerging technologies and trends in e-commerce, such as AI, AR, VR, voice commerce, and omnichannel retailing. Invest in technology solutions that streamline operations, enhance the customer experience, and drive growth.

Deliver personalized shopping experiences that cater to the individual preferences and needs of customers. Leverage data analytics, AI, and machine learning to understand customer behavior, preferences, and purchase patterns, and tailor product recommendations, marketing messages, and promotions accordingly.

Embrace sustainability and ethical practices throughout your supply chain, from sourcing and production to packaging and shipping. Consider offering eco-friendly products, using recycled materials, and minimizing waste and carbon emissions. Communicate your commitment to sustainability and ethics transparently to customers, and actively engage them in your efforts.

The e-commerce landscape is constantly evolving, and businesses must remain agile and adaptive to navigate changes and challenges. Continuously monitor industry trends, consumer behavior, and competitive dynamics, and be prepared to pivot and adjust your strategies accordingly.

As technology continues to reshape the e-commerce industry, investing in talent and skills development is crucial for staying competitive. Hire employees with the necessary expertise in areas such as data analytics, digital marketing, and technology, and provide ongoing training and development opportunities to keep their skills up to date.

Final Thoughts and Next Steps

As you reflect on your journey through the world of drop shipping and e-commerce, it's essential to take a moment to recap your accomplishments, acknowledge your challenges, and consider your next steps. Throughout this journey, you've likely encountered highs and lows, experienced moments of triumph and setbacks, and learned valuable lessons along the way.

Take a moment to reflect on how far you've come since embarking on your entrepreneurial journey. Consider the milestones you've achieved, the goals you've reached, and the obstacles you've overcome. Celebrate your successes, no matter how small, and acknowledge the hard work, dedication, and perseverance that have brought you to this point.

Think about the challenges you've faced along the way— the doubts, fears, and uncertainties that may have tested your resolve. Recognize that setbacks are a natural part of the entrepreneurial journey and an opportunity for growth and learning.

As you contemplate your next steps, remember that the path to success is rarely linear. It's okay to pivot, adapt, and course-correct along the way. Stay open to new opportunities, ideas, and possibilities, and be willing to take calculated risks to pursue your goals.

Stay true to your vision, your values, and your passion for what you do. Let your passion drive you forward, fuel your creativity, and inspire you to innovate and differentiate yourself in the marketplace. Stay focused on providing value to your customers, solving their problems, and exceeding their expectations with every interaction.

Remember that success is not just about reaching a destination—it's about embracing the journey, the growth, and the evolution that come with it. Stay committed to lifelong learning, personal development, and continuous improvement, both professionally and personally.

As you embark on the next phase of your journey, set clear goals, establish a strategic plan, and take deliberate action to move closer to your vision of success. Break down your goals into manageable tasks and milestones and hold yourself accountable for making progress each day. Stay disciplined, organized, and focused on your priorities, and be prepared to adjust your plans as needed to stay on course.

Above all, trust in yourself and your abilities, and believe in the value that you bring to the world through your business. You have the passion, the drive, and the determination to achieve your dreams, and with persistence and resilience, you can overcome any obstacle that stands in your way. Embrace the challenges, the opportunities, and the adventures that lie ahead, and seize the opportunity to make your mark on the world through your entrepreneurial journey.

CONCLUSION

"Mastering Drop Shipping Business: Building a Successful Online Retail Empire." Throughout this journey, you've gained a comprehensive understanding of the drop shipping model and learned how to leverage its advantages to create a thriving online retail business. As you reflect on the knowledge and insights gained from this book, let's recap some key takeaways and consider the next steps in your entrepreneurial journey.

Throughout the chapters of this book, you've delved deep into every aspect of the drop shipping business, from market research and niche selection to supplier management, e-commerce platform setup, and marketing strategies.

As you move forward on your drop shipping journey, remember the importance of continuous learning and adaptation. The e-commerce landscape is constantly evolving, with new technologies, trends, and consumer behaviors shaping the industry.

Lastly, don't forget the power of community and collaboration. Connect with other entrepreneurs, join online forums and communities, and seek mentorship from experienced professionals in the e-commerce space. By sharing insights, exchanging ideas, and learning from each other's experiences, you can accelerate your growth and overcome challenges more effectively.

As you embark on the next phase of your drop shipping journey, remember that success is not defined by overnight riches or instant fame. It's about building a sustainable business that brings value to your customers and enables you to achieve your goals and dreams.

Thank you for buying and reading/ listening to our book. If you found this book useful/ helpful please take a few minutes and leave a review on the platform where you purchased our book. Your feedback matters greatly to us.